Reckless
Faith

a 40-day journey
to saying yes

Reckless Faith

BETH GUCKENBERGER

Fedd Books
P.O. Box 341973
Austin, TX 78734

www.thefeddagency.com

Published in association with The Fedd Agency, Inc., a literary agency.

ISBN: 978-1-949784-16-9
eISBN: 978-1-949784-17-6

Printed in the United States of America

First Edition 15 14 13 12 11 / 10 9 8 7 6 5 4 3 2

To Emma, Evan, Josh, Aidan, Tyler, Marlen, Josh, Morgan, Marilin, Rory, Ari, Deedee, Carolina, Lupita, Olga, Gaby, and Todd.

Love makes a family.

contents

Introduction

It was two weeks before the *Reckless Faith* manuscript was due, and I was on a ten-day fast, finishing with what I hoped was Holy Spirit blessing. I was a first-time writer and had no systems or safeguards. I just lugged my heavy 2005 laptop around everywhere in Mexico, where my family and I were living as missionaries. I was in a parking lot, editing the final chapter while waiting for my son to finish a soccer practice. I could tell he didn't know where I parked, so I jumped out of the car to let him know where I was. A minute later, I returned to heartbreak.

Nooooo! Someone had smashed my window and stolen the laptop. They must have been watching me work, because the whole episode was executed in minutes.

I called my editor in the US and apologized. I never even *thought* about backing it up, I had never emailed it to myself, or stored it on a hard drive. It only lived in my head and on the stolen laptop. I told him, "I hardly had time to write it the first time, I definitely can't imagine rewriting it. Thank you, but I will not be able to fulfill our agreement." I am not sure what self-control he had to muster on his end, but somehow in a kind voice, he informed me I was under contract, and, while they would give me an extension, I was obliged to deliver what I had agreed.

I told everyone afterwards that the Enemy had taken it. I was sure what I had written was so Spirit-filled, he didn't want it out there edifying the body of Christ. I checked into a hotel the following weekend and wept as I redrafted the table of contents. *How am I going to remember all the stories I wrote? All that work!* I had no choice but to pray, and, as I offered up to God this assignment, He gently corrected me. I almost heard Him whisper, "*What if instead of what you want to tell them, you write about what I've told you?*" That was much easier, because I had been in God's classroom a long time, learning and being reintroduced to Him over and over again. I wrote until my hands cramped. Two days later, when my husband, Todd, picked me up, I told him the Enemy hadn't stolen that book. It was a branch needing to be cut off, as it wasn't going to bear any fruit.

I knew God had always been at work in the Ohio I grew up in, the same as the Mexico I was living in, but I just hadn't asked Him to show up as much or as big. I was busy getting smart in the ways the world told me to and taking care of my own needs, so I hadn't really needed to rely on

Him. We had moved to Mexico in 1997, with the intention of God using us to meet the needs of orphans, but it would be years before I realized God was more interested in loving me than using me. Today, we lead Back2Back Ministries, an international Christian non-profit organization dedicated to being a voice for orphans, but the lessons gathered from step one to today have been hard and vast. I learned the children we served, although orphaned, were no more in need of God than I was. There is an organization that's grown up underneath our feet, but it feels like a movement of people who are organized around pursuing the least of these (and getting found along the way). Todd and I have grown a large family in the meantime through biological, adopted, and foster care children who have taught us, like personal guides to our sanctification, what it means to die to self. All of my stories, children, and experiences have added up to a faith that's been tested over and over again. After ten years, I revisited the *Reckless Faith* stories that formed my faith and birthed this ministry, and reimagined them as devotionals. There's new content in here as well, as God is always teaching me when I am willing to learn. I've set up this devotional in a forty-day format, because *forty* is an important biblical number. Mentioned 146 times in Scripture, it generally symbolizes a period of testing and then renewal—think Moses and his *forty* years in Egypt, or the spies sent out for *forty* days. Think Jonah and *forty* days of warning Nineveh, and Elijah, who went *forty* days without food or water. Jesus was tested for *forty* days and appeared to the disciples for *forty* days until He ascended into Heaven.

Important pivots and decisions can be made in a forty-day time period, so I wanted us to walk together for those days and ask: *Where are you calling me, Lord, what are you trying to show me or say to me, and how can I respond to You with yes?*

In the start of 2018, I learned a new word that captivated me. *Hineni* is the Hebrew word translated as "Here I am." More accurately, it translates, "Whatever it is you are asking of me, I am already in agreement of it." It's used eight times in the Bible and each use occurs at defining moments in the biblical characters' lives, moments that required decision, action, and resolution, moments that required saying "yes" to God. Examples include, Moses saying "yes" when God called out to him to lead the Israelites out of slavery at the burning bush in Exodus 3, and Abraham saying "yes, here I am" when God called him to sacrifice his only son, Isaac, in Genesis 22. I want to have a spirit of *hineni*. Not count costs, not count myself out, but if God asked, led, or prompted, I want to respond with *yes*. There is one time in Scripture when the Lord says *hineni* actually *to* us:

Is not this the kind of fasting I have chosen: to loose the chains of injustice and untie the cords of the yoke, to set the oppressed free and break every yoke? Is it not to share your food with the hungry and to

provide the poor wanderer with shelter—when you see the naked, to clothe them, and not to turn away from your own flesh and blood?
Then your light will break forth like the dawn, and your healing will quickly appear; then your righteousness will go before you, and the glory of the LORD will be your rear guard. Then you will call, and the LORD will answer; you will cry for help, and he will say:
(hineni) Here am I.
– ISAIAH 58:6-9

There it is, the explanation of my whole Christian journey: busy about His work, in over my head, I needed Him to provide daily for what I didn't have in natural reserves. So, some days I asked for wisdom or discernment, some days for self-control or patience. I *hineni'd* my way through adoptions, friendships, tough assignments, marital fights, and health crises. What follows are several dozen stories of moments when God responded, each time saying "Here am I" and asking me to say "yes" to an ever-evolving reckless faith.

How This Book Works

"This is the best mountaintop experience, ever!" visiting, teen-aged Ashley exclaimed on the last day of her mission trip in Mexico. She meant to be encouraging, but I was crushed. If this short-term mission trip was a "mountaintop experience," that implied tomorrow, when she went home, she would begin the long spiritual descent. I wanted this trip to be a springboard for her future growth. Later that night, I was thinking more about the idea of experiences and how we can live through photographs and memories, or we can invite God in and be eternally changed. I began writing down these thoughts:

Experience: *I want people to have life-altering experiences.*
Reflection: *I want time for them to reflect on those experiences and wonder about themselves, others, and God.*
Change: *When good reflection happens, internal change is inevitable.*
Action: *That change leads to external actions, as we pursue God.*

I formed them into a circle so they looked like a clock.

If people have experiences, and they take the time to reflect on them, there's no limit to the transformation God can do. We are so wired to value experiences and take them as a sign of spiritual connection. As if the highest goal is to *feel* God. But what if we intentionally build in reflection time? What if we ask ourselves these questions: *What did I learn today about myself? Others? God?* What if we ponder the stories God walks us into? What kind of room would that create for maturity to develop?

Then after reflection, the natural progression is change. We could be *changed* after reflecting on those experiences, to be more like God—more loving, generous, joyful, discerning . . . the list is endless. Those changes could result in us living, doing, giving, and being more like Him. Those actions then spur on more experiences, and instead of those experiences becoming transient mountaintop experiences, they now become a circle of growth!

That conversation with Ashley took place over twenty years ago, and I can testify to its life-changing impact. I now look for experiences, little challenges throughout my day, that force me to step out of the comfortable and be propelled into a new, little storyline I wouldn't have asked for on my own. The discipline of reflecting on those experiences leads me to process through my day, learning more about myself and God. Reflection leads to growth and change—not the drastic "before and after" change we are used to seeing on television, but more of a "shift" to be who I was made to be. The internal change, or shift, results in external actions that will lead to more experiences, reflection, and change. It means I can't ever get away with saying "I feel stuck." I know exactly how to jumpstart my faith life—seek out experiences and get ready to do some reflection. The rest just becomes momentum.

What you have in your hands are some of my stories—experiences that perpetuated growth and change for me. I hope they might encourage you that God has lessons embedded into the smallest details of your day. There are daily challenges mentioned as a suggestion to put into action the principle illustrated. If another action inspires you, do it. It's not a prescription, it's a prompt to say *yes*.

We'll spend the next forty days looking for opportunities to say *yes* to God, and it's my prayer that, forty days later, you'll feel alive, connected, challenged, and free. After a biblical forty of anything, there is renewal. Days on an ark, weeks in a womb, years in a desert . . . I am hoping if we spend forty days journeying together, praying, listening, challenging ourselves, being encouraged, resting, there will be an inevitable transformation and renewal. It's my prayer you take up these forty days with a friend. Friends have shaded me throughout my whole life, bringing me comfort, truth when I needed it, encouragement, and strength. Friends hold us accountable and cheer on our victories. They stick with us in adversity. They aren't afraid of our questions and fears.

1

Rest is a Weapon
Yes to Still

I was asked by my pastors to teach one Sunday in a series called "What Jesus Invites Us To." I readily agreed. Then they said my Sunday would cover "Jesus Invites Us to *Rest,*" and I laughed out loud. I have never been good at rest. I accepted the challenge and jumped into the study, immediately looking up "rest." According to early translations from Hebrew to Greek, there is a word, *heschazo* that means to rest, to be quiet, to be still. It's found in the Septuagint, and while those translators aren't considered infallible, their scholarship does offer insight. I found *heschazo* in Genesis 4, and my mind raced to understand. I was familiar with the passage, having used it to teach on generational sin, but had no idea of its complete meaning.

> *Then the LORD said to Cain, "Why are you angry? Why is your face downcast? If you do what is right, will you not be accepted? But if you do not do what is right, sin is crouching at your door; it desires to have you, but you must rule over it."*
>
> – GENESIS 4:6-7 (EMPHASIS MINE)

I historically have taught this passage as: we all have sin crouching at our doors, based on our individual experiences and childhoods. Exposure to sin at a vulnerable age or stage makes the sin at our own doors appealing. But when I found *heschazo* in the middle of this passage, it hit me in a fresh way. It could be understood as, "If you do what is right/*heschazo* (if you are resting, if you are quiet, if you are still), will you not be accepted? But if you do not do what is right (if you are not resting, are not quiet, are not still), then sin is crouching at your door; it desires to have you, but you must rule over it."

Suddenly, the idea of rest shifted from a "time-out" (which I have never liked) to being a weapon I could use in my war against sin. Could God be inviting me into a rhythm where *He* is my deep breath? Could time in rest fortify me for the world I am fighting against and the life He's called me to? Could rest in Him be a sign not of weakness or tapping out but of strength and gearing up? Could rest be about not a lack of activity, but instead a still heart?

The week I was writing the sermon, I sat at my son Aidan's basketball game. I watched the time-outs, quarter breaks, half-time, and subbing in and out of players. I realized if the players didn't come out of play and rest, their performance would get sloppier over time. The coach saw intermittent rest as a way to strengthen and sustain them in the game. Could it be the same with God?

I love studying the Bible and all its nuance and complexity, but, in the end, it's pretty much summed up in two words: *come* and *go*. God has invited us into a relationship with Him, "Come to me" (Matthew 11:28), "Come to the waters" (Isaiah 55:1). The Spirit says "come" over and over again, and we are to come. The second word is "go." "Go into all the world" (Matthew 16:15), "Go, stand and speak" (Acts 5:20, KJV). There's a rhythm of coming and going, and if we just come and don't go, we miss the opportunity to fulfill God's will through our lives, but if we just go and don't come, we miss the opportunity to be filled by God and know Him. Rest and renewal is an invitation to fully experience all He offers us.

Our sins are different, but what we have in common is, without rest we are more at risk of being overcome. Healing from sin, pain, injury, wrong thinking, all happens in the margins, and I am increasingly aware of the critical role that rest plays. When I am living without rest, I risk burnout and lack motivation to stay in step with the Spirit.

One afternoon, I was having a hard moment with one of my sons. He was a newly adopted teenager and his will and mine were at odds. I called a friend, wanting some piece of magic advice to turn around my attitude and make him do what I wanted. Instead of advice, she said to me, "Take a beat, sit down, breathe . . ." She understood this principle: resting would strengthen me for the conflict I was facing and the sin that desired to overtake me.

Filling up is important, because then it allows us to pour out. We can give away what we just received (mercy, grace, wisdom, joy, love) because we know how to tap into the unending source. Isaiah 32:2 says, "Each one will be like a shelter from the wind and a refuge from the storm, like streams of water in the desert and the shadow of a great rock in a thirsty land." That "each one" means us! We can rest in His shelter, under His wing, and in His shade. He gives us rest, because He knows what we are going through and wants to be the place we run. Retreating in Him prevents us from escaping from life. Escape leads to disconnection, whereas retreating in Him leads to growth. Then, He asks us to extend to others what He has given us. From the rest we receive, we serve and we give to each other and to a world lost without Him.

Activity is my default, but activity without direction is just harried. I want to say *yes* to still, which isn't the same as "stop." It's a *yes* to purpose and priority, over bustle and busy.

REFLECTION:

Each one will be like a shelter from the wind and a refuge from
the storm, like streams of water in the desert and the
shadow of a great rock in a thirsty land.
– ISAIAH 32:2

What does this truth tell you about yourself? Others? God?

CHANGE:

How do you view rest? Who has provided shelter for you
in the past?

ACTION:

Find a tree or an overhang that provides shade and stand
underneath. Say a prayer, thanking God for who He has
used to shelter you.

2

A Long Way from
Sunday Lane
Yes to Questions

EXPERIENCE:

I am a long way from Sunday Lane. I stifle a laugh. There is nothing funny about where I am now, but laughing makes me less fearful. On my childhood street, I learned how to climb trees, how to make chocolate chip cookies, and how to drive. Riding down that street on my bicycle, I had a hunch not everyone lived like my family did, but I never could have imagined a street like the one I now find myself on.

I was now standing on a multi-lane roadway in Tirana, Albania, with every vehicle imaginable rushing by.

I see a little boy. What causes me to notice the little boy, I don't know, but there he was, seemingly lifeless, lying face down on the cobblestone. As I reach down, I see he is a toddler, but before I can lift him, a soldier points a machine gun at me and orders me to back up.

My fiancé, Todd, says "Beth . . . listen to him. I'm going to get the translator." He walks backwards, never breaking our gaze. It's 1994, and we are serving with Campus Crusade for Christ over our college spring break. I haven't even learned how to ask for water in Albanian, so negotiating with this officer seems impossible. I *do* know the key phrases of the Four Spiritual Laws, but he doesn't look receptive.

The officer seems relieved when the translator arrives. "The boy is property of the gypsies," the translator explains what the officer is saying. "They keep him awake all night so he'll sleep in the streets all day. People walk by and throw money at him, which the gypsies collect when they come to get him at dusk."

Why do the authorities allow this? I wonder. *Does the officer know the boy's caretaker? Perhaps he shares in the spoils?*

"It's too dangerous for him to be just left here." I say. Then I ask, "What stops me—or anybody—from picking him up and walking away with him? What stops me from doing something to help this child?"

* * *

Learn to do good; Seek justice, Reprove the ruthless, Defend the orphan, Plead for the widow.
– ISAIAH 1:17 (NASB)

This passage moves me. The rest of what you have in your hands is how these truths have played out in my life. For a long time, I hesitated even writing this book, wondering whether I could really make it worthy of a subject that's so important to me—the subject of reckless faith. While I long to love and give recklessly, I admit there are days when I don't. But the idea captivates me.

What I don't want is a "refined faith." Refined can mean "purified" but that is not the definition I am talking about. *Refined* can also be defined as "cultivated" and "fastidious." This "refined faith" is the opposite of the reckless faith I am writing about here. It's predictable and resistant to change. It pretends to know what God will do a hundred Sundays from now. It's more comfortable with rules, consequences, and baby steps. It likes control and people who agree. It fears what it can't see.

A truly reckless faith expects change and uncertainty and, as a result, it is eager to risk *more* and fear *less*! It knows there is more to the story, more than I experience now. A reckless faith always has one foot in eternity. It measures people by their actions and not their belongings. It believes when there is no evidence, and hopes in what is promised. It does not make sense to the world, and yet, the world often seems fascinated by it.

. . .

The Albanian officer keeps looking at me as I eye his machine gun. Through the translator, he finally answers my question: "Well, first, if you took the child away, you'd be taking him away from his legal caretaker; she'd probably just place another child here. Nothing would change. Second, it's the only life he has ever known. What else would he do?" He shrugs and turns around, dismissing me. He has bigger concerns than the boy and this curious tourist.

Todd and I sit on a park bench nearby and watch the boy sleep for the better part of an hour. *What else would he do?* keeps rolling around in my mind. I pray for the child, and his mother, I pray for my questions and the anger I feel. I pray for his country and the other children like him, certain to be lying on their own street corners. And then I pray I might have a hand in helping children like him.

Todd and I take a picture of him and talk about what we can do. Something shifts inside us. It's as though the wind is blowing, and we aren't sure from where it is coming but we can see the leaves kicking up. Something is rising in us, but we don't have the words to express it.

The next day, we visit our first orphanage, filled with children like the boy in the street. I sit on a concrete step on the second floor with a child on each knee and I feel as though the wind has stopped. There's a stillness I feel that's hard to explain. It isn't the stillness of inactivity, it is the calm of peace. I have more questions than answers, but in a place as foreign to Sunday Lane as I could've imagined, I feel as though I'm home.

REFLECTION:

Listen carefully: Unless a grain of wheat is buried in the ground, dead to the world, it is never any more than a grain of wheat. But if it is buried, it sprouts and reproduces itself many times over. ***In the same way, anyone who holds on to life just as it is destroys that life. But if you let it go, reckless in your love, you'll have it forever, real and eternal.*** *If any of you wants to serve me, then follow me. Then you'll be where I am, ready to serve at a moment's notice. The Father will honor and reward anyone who serves me.*

– JOHN 12:24-26 (MSG, EMPHASIS MINE)

What truth does this tell you about yourself? Others? God?

CHANGE:

What situations have you seen or heard about that leaves you uncomfortable or with questions? When and where have you felt most spiritually "at home?"

ACTION:

Find a picture of a person or a place you feel drawn towards. Hang it where you can see it every day and begin praying for clarity on what might be next.

3

A Burr in My Saddle

Yes to a New Direction

EXPERIENCE:

It's almost the end of the week, and we've run out of projects, supplies, and motivation. For the past few years, Todd and I have been adult chaperones in our church's youth mission trips to Queretaro, Mexico. In general, we know what to expect. A little paint here, a little polish there, some late-night tacos, an evangelistic drama—all in the name of the Lord.

As I unpack the paints on the fifth day of our trip, I complain to Todd, "Haven't we painted this wall before?" We are frustrated, the students are uninspired, and—worst of all—the nationals we have come to serve are unaffected by our efforts.

"Remember the orphanage we visited in Albania?" he asks, "You think there are any in this town?" I have no idea, but I am dying to get out of the paint project. We leave the kids in the hands of other responsible adults and we jump in a taxi cab.

Looking back now, it seems foolish. We didn't speak Spanish, didn't have much money if we got into trouble, and we were in a city where we could have easily gotten lost. However, an hour later, the cab driver, having finally understood us with our broken Spanish, brought to a children's home.

Through some creative communication, we told them, "We have two hundred US dollars, twenty-five eager students, and a whole day left in our trip. What would you do with those resources?" The man slowly responded, "The kids haven't had meat in over a year, and the front windows are broken. You can do something about that if you want."

The next day, we returned to the children's home with two hundred hamburgers, a new window, and our crew of teenagers. We set up the grill in the courtyard and served the meal. After all forty of the kids received their hamburgers and second helpings, we found ourselves still flipping burgers. Todd leans over to me, "What do you think is going on? These kids can't still be hungry; see if you can figure out where all the food's going."

I follow a preschool girl, who came up for her fifth

burger, up the stairs to the dormitory. With each step, it's almost as if I can feel her leading me, wanting me to see something. When we reach the top, she hesitates only slightly as she enters, and together, with the other preschoolers, I see them helping to lift up each other's mattresses, hiding hamburgers underneath, saving them for another day.

I call for Todd to join me and something happens to us that we don't even fully realize at the time. But when I chart the following events of my life, they trace back to that moment in the doorway of the orphanage. Those hidden hamburgers were a defining moment for us—an experience that impacted our thinking, touched our hearts, and compelled us into a new course of action. It changed our lives. I used to be afraid of the word *change,* as if it implied, somehow, I needed correction. But now I have a different view of change. It is a "shift" in perspective, a shift in what we think we are capable of, in where we want to see our life heading, in how we are willing to spend our time, talents, and resources.

The shift propelled us to step in a new direction we couldn't have taken on our own. Sometimes defining moments result in immediate and complete life transformations, like it did in Acts 9 for the apostle Paul on the road to Damascus, but more often such moments are subtle things we can only see in hindsight. For me, the hamburger incident was not a defining moment lit up in neon lights. I flew home the next day, went back to work, headed to the grocery store, and called my friends—but something was different. I have since described it as being like a burr under my saddle. As hard as I tried, I couldn't feel quite comfortable again in the same seat.

Before the trip to Mexico, I was not a bad person. I wasn't doing anything wrong that required major discipline in my life. But that trip was like a big wooden marker in the shape of an arrow pointing to someplace I couldn't see—a place I was nervous about, but also excited to explore. Just a week before the trip, the path I was on in my life had seemed fine, but now, in light of this experience, I didn't want *fine* anymore. For a year afterward, I moved around on the saddle, but there was always that silly burr reminding me I had changed in Mexico.

That is what reckless faith does—it propels us faster and harder towards God's true plan for our lives. Todd and I talked hundreds of hours in the following year about those hamburgers. *What could we do?* It became clear that the arrow was pointing us back to Mexico, and so, without much guidance other than a vague sense of the rightness of the decision, in 1997, we moved to Monterrey, Mexico.

Today, when people look at the organization and ask us about strategy, vision casting, projection, and planning, we just smile. It would be tempting to spin it all so it seems more polished, or we seem more sophisticated. But the truth is, it started with a little girl hiding a hamburger under her mattress, and us saying *yes* to a new direction.

REFLECTION:

Have I not commanded you? Be strong and courageous. Do not be afraid; do not be discouraged, for the LORD your God will be with you wherever you go.
– JOSHUA 1:9

What does this truth tell you about yourself? Others? God?

CHANGE:

When have you been shifted? What area of your life are you feeling a burr under your saddle?

ACTION:

Sketch a quick timeline of your life. Record the dates and places God used as trajectory-changing moments in your life. Pray and thank Him for how He moves us.

4

One Foot in Eternity

Yes to Sacrifice

One of my first lessons in reckless faith came from a man named Pepe. He and his wife, Lucy, became believers in adulthood. They had children, a house, and employment. Many evenings, as they watched the nightly news together, they would hear reports on crimes committed in an area in downtown Monterrey called *La Coyotera*.

One evening, a newscaster reports that even the police were afraid to go into this community, and, as a result, it was a favorite hangout for criminals. Pepe decides he can't watch the news anymore, he has to act. He takes a bus into the *centro* and sits down in a bar in the heart of *La Coyotera*.

When he returns home later that evening, he is so excited—not that anything happened, but he felt a rush in his spirit and a desire to return. Return he does, night after night, sharing his faith with the men in the bar and outside on the streets. Eventually, he forms a relationship with the bar owner, whom he leads to the Lord.

One night while they're talking, the bar owner asks Pepe, "What would you do if you had this building?"

"What do you mean?" Pepe asks.

"I mean, if this wasn't a bar where men could come and forget about their problems. What would you do here for the men in this community? How would you help them forget about their lives and struggles?"

Pepe promises to pray about that question and goes home to share it with his wife. Less than a year later, on the site where Pepe had first come to see *La Coyotera*, he opens a mission. In the morning, men come to receive a hot breakfast while they hear him share about not forgetting their lives, but finding true purpose in Jesus Christ. Good news travels fast, and Pepe's mission is no exception. He quickly outgrows his little building and moves to a new building. A group of formerly homeless and jobless men now work for him, making food, cleaning up the building, following up with people who visit. They function much like an elder or deacon board.

By the time we meet Pepe on his street corner, with a big black Bible in his hands, his mission occupies most of the city block. He has a church across the street from the original mission and a home where men and women can get the help they need to break free from drug addiction. I love going to Pepe's church. Most days he has open mic—and there are some R-rated testimonies of how God saved prostitutes, gang members, deadbeat dads, and glue sniffers.

One night, Zeke, a visiting friend, asks us if his mission team can spend the night down at Pepe's church to help out with the increased number of people who show up once the sun goes down. I call Pepe. He weighs the risks but says, "If God is calling them to come tonight, it's because He has a reason for it." Our group goes down there to work, serve, pray, and clean. At bedtime, Pepe makes sure the team is settled in for the night, then he goes outside, closes the door behind him, and, without drawing any special attention to himself, lays down in front of the church door and sleeps on the street. If anyone wants to break in and hurt the Americans, they'll literally have to move Pepe first.

Pepe died a few years ago. Old age and a battle against illness finally claimed him. He is now in our great "cloud of witnesses" (Hebrews 12:1). I know we can't see or hear those witnesses, but their lives still tell us amazing stories. Noah's story teaches us to listen even when what we hear doesn't make sense. Abraham's story says God is always "on time." And Pepe's story tells us it is always important to take the first step, because that's how every journey starts.

Some of those who heard Pepe preach were able to take their first steps out of addiction, others heard him and took their first steps toward reconciliation. Pepe could have lived the last two decades of his life in greater luxury—with more security and fewer complications—and he would still be in heaven and in communion with God. But I can hear him saying, "Betty (that's what he called me), keep one foot in eternity. This world is not our home." His life was a technicolor lesson for me in sacrifice, the faith and sacrifice of biblical heroes come to life.

Pepe made an impact in the lives of hundreds of people because he lived life with a reckless faith. He breathed spiritual confidence into those around him. He was not a great preacher, nor was he able to pray eloquently. He was not a gifted fundraiser for his mission. Another person might have been great at all those things and still had a lackluster ministry, bearing little fruit and encouraging complacency. Pepe was good at one essential thing: he trusted God had a purpose for his life and said *yes* to sacrificing towards it. As a result, God took care of the rest. There were always tamales for the morning outreach, and there were always people who came to hear him preach—all because one night he shut off the TV and walked into a bar.

REFLECTION:

Therefore, since we are surrounded by such a great cloud of

witnesses, let us throw off everything that hinders and the sin that so easily entangles. And let us run with perseverance the race marked out for us.
– HEBREWS 12:1

What does this truth tell you about yourself? Others? God?

CHANGE:

What are you willing to sacrifice? What are you not willing to sacrifice? What might the world find crazy that God keeps nudging you toward?

ACTION:

Whose voice is in your head, cheering you on towards righteousness? Write them a letter and thank them (even if they are now in heaven). Include in your letter how you are passing along their inspiration as a witness to others.

5

He is Not a Genie God
Yes to Healing

EXPERIENCE:

God put adoption on my heart long before I was ever married. During our first year in Mexico, Todd and I tried for most of the year to adopt a set of sisters, but halfway through the process, it fell apart. I was full of pain and questions.

A year later, the money we had saved had run out, and we headed home from Mexico to organize ourselves and raise support to return. We had arrived the year before as a couple, but were now leaving as a family of three, having given birth to our daughter Emma. Some friends decided to stay in our little rental house in downtown Monterrey while we were in America, furthering the ministry efforts.

Upon return, Todd started a job at a local Christian school. On the first day of classes, while home with Emma, I got an urgent call for help from our friends in Mexico. A little girl we loved in one of the orphanages had been hit by a car.

"Go to this hospital . . . ask for this doctor . . ." I was giving instructions, but couldn't figure out how to get them the needed funds. Irrationally, I promised, "You know what? I'll fly out on the noon flight and be there by dinner with the money. See you soon."

I then left Todd a note on the kitchen table, "Running to Mexico with Emma. Ruth's been hit by a car. See you this weekend. Love you."

Emma and I fly to Mexico and go straight to the hospital. Afterwards, we return to our old home, where our friends are now living. The phone rings. "*Bueno*," I answer. It was a woman looking for me, and, by God's sovereignty, I was in Mexico to answer the phone even though I shouldn't have been there, as I didn't live there anymore. If my friends had answered the phone, they wouldn't have understood her. She was looking for an American family who had paperwork ready and was interested in adopting a baby from another Mexican state *the next day at noon.* Even though I had more questions than answers, I knew. The answer was *yes.* After writing down the details, I hung up and called Todd. Despite feeling overwhelmed, we had this moment where we invited the Holy Spirit to give us the peace-that-passes-understanding. It made no sense, but it felt very right in the right places of our hearts.

The next day, we met our son Evan, and I knew immediately that something was wrong. His current weight was lower than his birth weight, and it was easy to see why. He struggled to eat, remained rigid in our arms, had trouble sleeping, and panted like he couldn't catch his breath. His legs were scissored and his arms twisted in a frozen position, he had a rash all over him. Todd and I were overwhelmed with love and concern for our new son. We were confused, overjoyed, afraid, and prayerful—all at the same time.

Seven weeks later, after the adoption was complete, we headed back to Cincinnati. Doctor visits for Evan started right away, and eventually I sat with his neurologist for the results. He began, "Your son will never walk."

I sat stunned as Evan played on my lap. The neurologist continued, "Your son has profound cerebral palsy. The faster you accept him the way he is, the better it is for this child. Whatever you were thinking when you adopted him, replace it now with the reality that you have a special-needs son."

The doctor didn't know what he was doing, but he was stepping on my spiritual bruise—that spot in your heart where you've been disappointed by people and circumstances, and you've assigned that disappointment to God. My bruise came from my father's death several years before. He had cancer, and I had begged God to heal him.

I wondered hopelessly as I listened to the doctor, *How do I pray? Does God even heal?*

When I arrived home that afternoon, my tears had dried, but Todd came home and they started again. We prayed and watched our two babies sleeping together. Emma curled into a ball, relaxed and peaceful. Evan crinkled along one side of his crib—his left hand sticking into the air at an awkward angle, a reminder of his condition.

A tremendous shift happens when a gnawing fear becomes confirmed: hope temporarily dies. Then hope is reborn in the form of faith, faith that God will take over, even if I can't yet see how. We dove into the therapy circuit—occupational, physical, water, and sensory therapy, and all the while I tried to hold onto faith, even in moments of doubt.

A year passed and a therapist came to the house, accusing me of rescuing Evan too much. Her words: "You need to let him struggle more." I called her crazy. His every moment was a struggle, why let him struggle more? Later that day, Emma grabbed a toy out of Evan's hand and walked quickly across the room. Evan cried for it, and I joined him. Lost in my own tears (*Are we ever moving back to Mexico? Is he ever getting better? Did Dad have to die?*), I almost missed him struggling to get across the room on his belly. He had never moved like that before, and, just stunned, I watched him pull up onto the couch and "cruise" across it. I remember being in shock and yet aware that what I was seeing was supernatural. When the couch ended, he stepped forward. I gasped. A step. Then another. The tears now blurring my view. He's *walking*.

I drove like a wild woman to Todd at work. *Did I even buckle the kids in?* I set Evan on the ground, and he toddled over to his dad. We were speechless, grateful, and humbled. We talked about wedding aisles and soccer fields, and made plans to return to Mexico. Evan's one step became a hundred more. Soon he was running and playing on soccer teams. Today, he is a healthy wide receiver for his college football team and has no trace of cerebral palsy. It was a miraculous healing.

I had the privilege of sharing his testimony at his university chapel, and the students roared when he walked on stage. I told them, "The reason we share isn't so you know something wildly personal about our family. It's to testify that with God all things are still possible."

Today I think about how I prayed to the same God for two men I loved. One of those stories turned out nothing like I wanted, and the other turned out better than I ever imagined. God healed me, too, when I knelt before His sovereignty and confessed: *You are not a genie god, made in my image, who grants me wishes.* My bruise finally healed when I accepted that I am made in God's image, and I committed to submit my will to His way.

If He wrote the story, I can trust it's good.

REFLECTION:

Now to him who is able to do infinitely more than we ask or imagine, according to his power that is at work within us, to him be the glory in the church and in Christ Jesus throughout all generations, for ever and ever! Amen.
— EPHESIANS 3:20-21

What does this truth tell you about yourself? Others? God?

CHANGE:

What are your spiritual bruises? Where and what can you ask Him for healing today?

ACTION:

Find a Band-Aid and write down the name of a disappointment in life that can still feel bruised to you. Wear it throughout the day and ask God for healing from it.

6

Do You Love Him?
Yes to Testify

One day, when we were living in Mexico, a young woman came to my door minutes before I was headed out to the zoo with Emma and Evan. I needed a mental break from my responsibilities and I had planned on an afternoon of play. "*No sé*," she says as she lets out the big breath she's been holding, "They told me to come here and talk to you, but I do not know where to start." I wrestled down the irritation my flesh feels when there's an interruption. This girl looks young, vulnerable, and like she could benefit from a day at the zoo as much as I could.

"I'm on my way out . . ." I glance down at her swollen abdomen, "But why don't you come with us, and we can talk about whatever is on your mind while we walk around?"

Throughout the afternoon, she shares her story with me. She shares that she broke a glass Coke bottle earlier in the week and swallowed the pieces, hoping to rid her body of a baby she had conceived during an unwanted sexual episode.

My heart broke for her. Vulnerability is a funny thing, almost contagious if we allow it. Her vulnerability seemed connected to bravery, and the more she offered it, the more I was eager to help her. "Well, lesson number one," I say, "your reproductive organs and digestive tract are not connected. The baby isn't really *in* your belly."

Evan interrupts us the way preschoolers do, pointing at the lions through the fence. "Lions! Stay here Mommy, please; I want to watch them."

The young woman looks at me strangely and swivels her head back and forth between me and my Mexican son, "He speaks *English?*"

"Yes," I explain, "my husband and I adopted him as a baby, so his first language is ours. I hope he'll learn Spanish one day, but for now it's *Mommy*, not *Mamá.*"

The rest of the day she listens as I talk about her options for her unborn baby, but she later would tell me it was all background noise. She couldn't stop watching and listening to Evan.

"Let's get together at the end of the week after you've

had some time to think. Why don't we meet again on Friday? Do you have any questions for me about what we talked about today?" We had covered a lot, and I wanted her to fully understand her choices.

"Yes, I do have one." She looked down at my double stroller. "Do you love him like you do her?" she said, pointing to our biological daughter.

Stunned, I asked, "That's your question? Not about the medical issues we discussed, or the spiritual truths, or the practical concerns, or your care, or abortion, or adoption, or protection, or the legal items we covered; after all of all that, you want to know if I love my son like a son?" I'm incredulous.

"Yeah," she said, looking me in the eye for the first time that afternoon. "I've never seen an adopted kid with his mother before. I'm just curious. *Do you love him?*"

I realize then that moments like this are why the Bible talks so much about love. It is powerful and can break through tremendous strongholds and absolutely fascinates a world that has never seen it.

"Yes" I laughed, "That one is easy. I love him. I love him like crazy. I couldn't love him more if I wanted to."

Six months later, she held my hand while she went into labor and delivered a little girl, whom she decided to place into the arms of adoptive parents. Now that little girl—who survived her mother's attempt to abort her with a broken Coke bottle—has a story of her own. Her life and testimony will go on to encourage her parents, future generations, and everyone who hears her story.

Once again, I learned that God has the right to use what He has built to draw others towards Himself. When we hear a testimony, we believe more, trust more, and have more confidence in the Author of our story. In a world where there is so much noise, so much talking at people, it's hard to find the quiet moment to really *say* something. And what do we end up saying? Careful words so as to not offend. In all our carefulness, are we missing the chance to exchange with others the lessons we've learned and questions we honestly have?

It's a reckless kind of faith that causes you to invite someone you don't know into conversation. This birth mama's fearlessness (to get in a car with me, to ask questions, to be curious about adoption) made a mark on me. When I feel in over my head, could I, like her, search out solutions and counsel from someone who lives so differently than me?

Shame wanted her to stay silent, to shrink back, and feel despair. Over the course of the rest of her pregnancy, we talked about life and hope, choices and the future. She felt confident and courageous on the day she handed over her daughter, when she could've felt anything but. She literally learned a new way of thinking and then acted on her new conviction in a way that blessed her baby, the adoptive parents, and herself (and me while watching).

When we invite God into the story, we can't always

predict the outcome—there isn't a formula, or an easy answer. But when we listen and step forward to say *yes*, we see Him as a Reconciler, Rebuilder, Redeemer, Restorer, and Repairer of all things. Some of those stories are messy and will never be resolved and tied with a bow, but a reckless faith shares without reserve how God has worked and then leaves the rest to Him.

REFLECTION:

A new command I give you: Love one another. As I have loved you, so you must love one another. By this everyone will know that you are my disciples, if you love one another.
– JOHN 13:34-35

What does this truth tell you about yourself? Others? God?

CHANGE:

How has God used your testimony to encourage someone to act or believe? Where have you seen a strong testimony of love that inspired you?

ACTION:

While you are out today, look for someone who is different than you (could be age, color, nationality, etc.). Make eye contact and smile at them. If appropriate, initiate a conversation with a simple observation or greeting. Take a moment to wonder about their day and experiences, and say a prayer that you might leave a good impression.

7

What a Mess I Had Made
Yes to His Strength

Squinting, I see shacks in every direction—homemade out of plastic, wood, scrap metal, broken block. I'm visiting the families inside to see if they have a special "Easter burden" we can pray for this morning. *Who am I kidding? Easter burden? Try daily burden,* I think as I see women washing clothes in a river and babies walking around without diapers.

"Mom, we haven't been down *that* road yet." Emma points to a little pathway leading toward the riverbank. Having already been to a dozen homes and hearing about more needs than I can ever conceive of helping, I am wearing down.

"Okay, one more," I say, "then some shade." I playfully tousle her hair. *Lord, give me some of that "glory strength."* It has been a season of feeling like we have more work to do than we can possibly accomplish, more children to reach out to than we have helpers, more funding needs than anyone can meet.

I walk down to the shacks lining the river. "*Buenos días,*" I cheerfully greet the little girl standing in the dirt. "Are your parents home?"

"Not now," she answers shyly, her eyes full of fear.

Not wanting to scare her, I try a different approach. "We're here to pray with anyone who wants to talk to God about the worries they may have. Do you have something you want to pray about?" She walks back to her door, which is only a sheet covering the entryway. *Was that an invitation?* Just as I am about to tell Emma we will pray here in front of the little house, the girl returns.

"*Sí*, I have something I am worried about," she says. "Will God do anything about it?"

"He is not a magician, so we can't ask Him for a trick, but we can share with Him how we are feeling and what we're afraid of, and He'll comfort us as we begin a relationship with Him. Would you like that?" She leads us into her one-room home. Inside are five small children, the youngest is in diapers. There is no food, and the lack of cleanliness makes me wonder how long my new young friend has been left in charge.

"We're hungry," she simply states. She doesn't ask for

her parents to return, or a bike, or a better house. She just wants food for herself and her siblings. I begin, *"Lord, would you bring nourishment for these children? Amen."*

Then I decide I can "fix" the problem. After promising we'll return, Emma and I walk to a nearby food stand, where I buy several days' worth of groceries. I hope this will be the answer to their prayers. We return and spend some time arranging the food on their makeshift table.

"I'm going to let the pastor know about your needs. I'll keep praying for you and for your mother's safe return. God bless you." I hug her. "And happy Easter." I feel good inside and so does Emma. We are leaving them in a better situation than we found them. As we walk away, I put Emma on my shoulders. When we're about a block away, Emma yells, "Mom, turn around, go back! There are people all around those kids' house!"

Sure enough, I hadn't even noticed we were being watched as we walked back to their home earlier, our arms full of groceries and my heart full of good intentions. All the neighbors knew those kids were alone, and now they've come to steal their food. By the time we reach the door of the shack, a number of very unfriendly people are milling around. Crying, the oldest girl looks accusingly and says, "Is this how God answers prayers?" Flustered by her question, and by the people standing around, I panic. *Oh God, what's going on? Please intervene!*

God certainly doesn't delight in our fear, but I do think

He sometimes politely waits to act until we've tried our own solution and failed.

What a mess I had made. To be honest, I wanted to be able to imagine those children filling their bellies so I would not feel so guilty about filling mine. *Lord, forgive me!* As I cry out in His name, my heart is flooded with peace. I know He's staking His claim over this shack. It feels like a wind blowing, but there's no movement in the trees. Where the Accuser had been just moments ago, stirring up fear and trouble, the army of angels is beginning to swoop in. One of the Enemy's favorite tricks is to fill the air with fear, but now, slowly, people begin to walk away. The *Prince of Peace* was here.

The children and I walk over to a woman in the community who is respected and knows everyone and everything. "These kids' *mamá* disappears for days at a time to work," she says as she scolds them, "Why didn't you come out sooner and ask for help?" She sets out some warm tortillas on the table. "I will keep an eye on them until their *mamá* comes home" she says. I nod in appreciation. The oldest girl, falling into a heap, begins to cry softly. Emma and I hug them goodbye, and I let this woman minister to them with an understanding of that life I do not share.

House by house, I gathered the community's Easter burdens in my own basket, trying to figure out how to fix everything until I lost sight of why I was there—to listen and love. Burden-carrying can do that to you—it clouds your vision.

I can feel sick for little ones who bear burdens they weren't meant to. I want to blame someone. Is it the government's fault? Society's? Their mothers'? The absentee fathers'? I want to blame the church. I'd like to say it's because of the economy or the war. But it's all of those reasons and none of those. God asks us to be present in hard stories, to make room for Him to heal. He asks us to listen and work with strength not our own. He will use us, not for the sake of the work, but for the chance to love. When I am tempted to carry what's not mine, I remember how easily I can make it worse without intending.

So, what's to be my response? Say *yes* to His strength, connect with others, listen, love well, and in doing so, lighten the burden in His name, and not my own.

REFLECTION:

As you learn more and more how God works, you will learn how to do your work. We pray that you'll have the strength to stick it out over the long haul—not the grim strength of gritting your teeth but the glory-strength God gives. It is strength that endures the unendurable and spills over into joy, thanking the Father who makes us strong enough to take part in everything bright and beautiful that he has for us.
– COLOSSIANS 1:9-12 (*MSG*)

What does this truth tell you about yourself? Others? God?

CHANGE:

Have you ever put energy towards building your own kingdom? When have you tried to fix something that wasn't yours to fix?

ACTION:

Place a heavy object in your pocket or purse to carry throughout the day. At the end of the day, take out the "heavy burden" and lay it at the feet of Jesus, thanking Him for being willing to carry what we can't. Then share about the burden you were carrying with a trusted friend who will encourage and pray for you.

8

He Looks at the Heart

Yes to Conviction

EXPERIENCE:

The phone rings late Friday afternoon. "Beth?" says a woman who works at a local orphanage. "It's Sandra. I'm glad I caught you. We have a young girl here who has a newborn baby she wants to drop off, but she doesn't have any paperwork. I can't accept her son until Monday morning when we get him a birth certificate, but I am afraid if I send her back out in the streets, we won't see her again. Can she and her baby stay with you for the weekend?"

Fifteen minutes later, they're at my door. I can hardly disguise my shock when I see how young this new mother is—*fourteen*. I lead her down the hall. "Here's your room." As she settles in, I try to figure out how to connect with her and penetrate her detached attitude.

"Do you want me to bathe your baby? Would you like him to sleep with us tonight?"

She seems grateful. After weeks of caring for her baby without anyone's help, she hands him over to me; then, exhausted, falls asleep. I stand in her doorway and wonder what is going on in her heart. She thought she would have to give her baby up today, but now she has two more days to spend with him. *Is she happy? Frustrated? Scared?*

In the morning, I am full of questions: "Who is the baby's father? Where are your parents? Where do you live?" Her answers are curt and tense. Her body language tells me to leave her alone. I turn my attention from the difficult mother to the adorable baby, who melts in my arms. "Caleb," I whisper in his ear, "God has a wonderful life for you and a future full of hope." This is exactly why I became a missionary to orphans, so I could tell them about God's love. Then I look up and see his mom, and the mood shifts. She is sassy, hard, and not easily engaged.

"Did you sleep okay?" I ask. "Hungry?"

"*Whatever.*"

"We have all day; what would you like to do?"

"*Whatever.*"

When I discover the baby has severe diaper rash and is malnourished, I struggle with judgmental feelings toward the mother. *Lord, in all the hours she's cared for him today, did she never once change his diaper?* Thankfully, God will not let me sit quietly in my sin. It takes no effort to look down on people. It's actually lazy. When I think of the people I have looked down on in the past, they are usually people whose lives I couldn't relate to. They lived in different times or places, and it was too much work for me to try to understand their point of view. Had God not allowed me to see life through this young mother's eyes, I might still have the question, *How did she get herself into this mess?*

Later that afternoon, I am waiting for another orphanage to come over for a cookout. With Caleb on my hip, I wander into the girl's room and say, "We're having some guests tonight. You don't have to help, but at the least come out and eat with us; it's the only dinner I'm serving tonight." She maintains her look of disinterest. Then a van pulls up and the kids from the visiting orphanage stream out the back. Caleb's mom comes out of her room and looks like she wants to say something, but before she can, the front door of the van opens. As I greet the orphanage director, I hear Caleb's mother's gasp behind me. I turn to see the problem, as she grabs Caleb and runs back to her room. I follow her, but she locked the door. I can hear her sobbing.

Soon we start our dinner. When I think I won't be noticed, I slip out and knock softly on her door. She yanks me inside, "Don't make me go out there," she says. "I grew up with that lady, and the last thing I want her to know is that she was right. I walked myself right into a trap."

"You grew up at that orphanage?" I ask in disbelief.

"Yes. I left a year ago, listening to the sweet talk of a boy I met each day after school and walked home with. Only one day, I didn't walk home. We just kept going and by the time I realized I was far from the orphanage, I was filled with such freedom I didn't care. About a month later, they found me and insisted I return. They made all sorts of threats if I didn't come with them then I wouldn't be able to come back at all. But by then I was addicted to what the boy was selling, and a month later I was pregnant."

I sit shocked. She is an orphan herself. *What does it feel like to have no model for a mother and yet to be one yourself?* Tears form as I realize the same promises I have been whispering to Caleb apply to her.

"He stopped showing me off once I was pregnant, so now I just clean up the house and make myself useful to whoever I can, if you know what I mean. I don't want this baby to grow up in that environment, and I don't trust what he will do to Caleb if he gets angry at the crying or at me. He doesn't want to be a father, but he is probably going crazy right now because I didn't come home last night. He will wonder where the baby is, and I don't know if even I can return there."

"I can't let her see me," she rambles on. "She was right, but I can't let her know that. I can't go back until I have my life straightened out. Please don't tell them I'm here."

In just five minutes' time, she has quadrupled the number of words that she has spoken all weekend, but this new vulnerability cracked open the door for me to begin ministering to her. First, it required I get off my throne of contempt and criticism. Now overwhelmed with the privilege I have to speak truth into a heart so broken, I am convicted beyond words for my judgmental thoughts.

On Monday, we deliver Caleb and his mother to an orphanage where she processes the baby's birth certificate. I whisper in Caleb's ear, not about the mother who gave him up, but about a woman who dreamed something better for him than she could offer herself, the woman who got in over her head and sought out Christians as a refuge for him as they had once been for her.

We don't all start out on the same block. We don't all get the same parents, houses, vacations, and educations in our lives. We don't get the same experiences; we don't have the same capacities or support systems. We generally do the best we can with what we are handed. Even if someone behaves differently than I would, I am still in no position to judge. Only a God who sees our life from the beginning through to the end has the right to judge us, and even He doesn't look at the outward appearances. He looks at the heart.

REFLECTION:

Why do you look at the speck of sawdust in your brother's eye and pay no attention to the plank in your own eye? How can you say to your brother, 'Let me take the speck out of your eye,' when all the time there is a plank in your own eye? You hypocrite, first take the plank out of your own eye, and then you will see clearly to remove the speck from your brother's eye.

– MATTHEW 7:3-5

What does this truth tell you about yourself? Others? God?

CHANGE:

Who and when are you most likely to judge? When do you feel self-condemnation?

ACTION:

Find a piece of wood and use a Sharpie to write down one of your sins. Place it on your desk, or in your car, somewhere you'll see it regularly as a reminder to work out your own faith before judging someone else's.

9

Your Mama Co-Labored
Yes to Pray

EXPERIENCE:

Todd and I have a large family full of biological, adopted, and aged-out foster children. It was never the intention, and I couldn't even begin to trace back how it all happened, but here we are now—a mess of people who love and are committed to each other. Two of those people we raised were our foster daughters, sisters we loved and battled for (for more than two decades). Our story with them has been chronicled in other places, but can be summed up with one word: *perseverance*. We have persevered through a failed adoption and long-term foster care. We persevered through one of them going through a rebellious adolescence and we are gratefully on the other side with a more mature young woman. We believed in and hoped for the redemption of a lost girl who finally came home emotionally and spiritually several years ago. Today, these sweet girls are treasures to us, but it was from this hope that one day everything would be great that I originally preached to myself, to the girls, to Todd, to the Lord, and to anyone else listening: "It doesn't matter what it looks like from here; *the story isn't over yet.*"

One hot Sunday, many summers ago, we sat in the open-air church at the top of the hill in my Mexican neighborhood, singing "*Te Doy Gloria.*" It was a loosely structured service, populated mostly with the children from the orphanage down the hill, unprogrammed as far as services go, but it takes me to a place of worship faster than many other places I have visited. The service finished and people lingered at the back before heading to their chicken stands and taco bars for lunch.

"Beth, do you have a minute?" I turned around to see a visiting guest, Mark, waiting for my answer.

"Oh sure, of course." I glanced around, quickly sizing up the patience level and approximate meltdown time of my children around me. I thought they had a few good minutes left in them. "What's going on?"

He started to tell me a story about his mother, Barbara—a woman I had never met, but when he said her name, it rang a bell. I remembered people mentioning her before in the context of prayer; she was known as an intercessory prayer warrior. "Barbara Shaw is praying for our trip" or "I'll pass this along to Barbara to pray for." All this was running through my mind, when Mark interrupted my thoughts to say, "She passed away this last year."

Oh. "I'm sorry for your loss."

"Someone a couple of years ago gifted her a painting from a collection at one of your fundraising banquets. Do you remember those?"

I remembered. Some young girl from the Midwest had contacted me, wanting to use her art skills for orphan care advocacy. I told her she could paint some canvases and sell them, sending us the proceeds. She readily agreed and asked me for a stack of photographs for the paintings she was going to sell. She chose some to copy onto canvas. Then we auctioned them off at our annual banquet that year.

Mark continued, "Someone bought one of those for my mom and it hung in her house, where she prayed for the two children in the painting on a regular basis. As she neared the end of her life, she told me that she wanted the painting to come into my home after she was gone and she wanted me to continue praying for the children. Something in her said there was more work to do, and she wasn't sure what that looked like on the 'other side,' so I gave my consent. Since she has passed, I have been praying regularly for the children, but I don't have my mom's gifts. I am not sure what to pray exactly, and I find myself saying the same thing over and over. So, I was hoping . . ." He paused, a pleading look on his face. "I took a picture of the painting and I brought it with me for you to look at. Could you give me some background on the kids, just so I can pray more specifically?"

I panicked inside. *Lord, what if I don't recognize them? It's been years, what if the children have moved on and I don't know them? I can tell it's important to him, Lord, help me know them!* After this internal panic, I nodded my agreement. "Show me the picture, and let me get my children, because they will know more of the kids collectively than I will. Let's see if between all of us, we can recognize them."

I called them all over and they moved to my side as he pulled out his picture. We all looked at it and stared, stunned. Tears filled my eyes, which were full of recognition.

Our foster daughters turned to me, burying their heads in each shoulder, and we all looked at each other and then back at him. "It's them, Mark. It's these two girls. We recognize the photograph it's been copied from."

He looked as wide-eyed as I did. The sweat beaded on my forehead as I wound up to preach to anyone within earshot, "Do you realize that your mama co-labored with us in the salvation of these girls' souls? The Great Shepherd loves them so much, that as He set out on the trail to seek the one sheep here separated from the flock of ninety-nine, He enlisted in the battle a prayer warrior from Ohio? She was actively engaged in orphan care without ever having set foot in this country. Now tell me, when exactly did she start praying?"

Comparing notes, I begin to recount for him the last couple years of their lives, specifically how God wooed the oldest to Himself a year and half prior to that. We looked at each other and I exclaimed, "Now back to your original question, get out your pen and paper. I have a long list of things for you to pray!"

REFLECTION:

So do not fear for I am with you; be not dismayed, for I am your God. I will strengthen you and help you; I will uphold you with my righteous right hand.
– ISAIAH 41:10

What does this truth tell you about yourself? Others? God?

CHANGE:

Who do you pray for? Who prays for you?

ACTION:

Set an alarm on your phone as a reminder to pray at a set time each day for a specific person (even if it's just two minutes!).

10

I Called in
Reinforcements

Yes to Bold

EXPERIENCE:

Years ago, after two of our foster daughters had settled into our family routine, an extended family member of theirs, who didn't seem to have their best interests in mind, came around threatening to disrupt our family unit. She was against our faith, nationality, and probably my hair color and shoe size. She was making a lot of noise that she was going to use their shared family heritage to have the girls removed and placed under her full-time care. In many situations, this would be an answer to prayer, but in this case, without going into detail, it was cause for great alarm.

The girls were worried, I was concerned, and those feelings together rose to panic level when this family member of theirs called one afternoon. She told me in no uncertain terms she was going to come the next Friday with the authorities and remove the girls from our home.

I knew once we could sort things out with any authority, they would see the stability the girls had experienced in our care, and would note the lack of involvement of any family of origin up until this point. Because of this, I wasn't worried about the long run; I was more worried about the interim and how traumatic it would be for them to be taken away. I called in reinforcements.

"Mama Martha" was the near saint who had raised the girls in her children's home until they had come to live with us. With her slow, articulate speech, her gray hair, and impeccable manners, I thought Martha would be my ace in the hole. Should someone come making false claims, she could set anyone straight.

I called her and asked, "Will you bring all your files on the girls: visitor logs their family never signed into, kindergarten records you had to fill out, yearly reports—anything and everything to show this latest 'interest' is not entirely sincere?"

"Of course, Beth" she answered, "I will bring what we need and be there beside you in case they follow up with their threats." I spent most of that week in government offices, amassing a strong case and evidence the girls needed to stay in our care.

Martha came to my home, as promised, shortly before we expected any trouble, and she patted her bag in response to my raised eyebrows, "I have everything we need." She smiled.

Then a small entourage pulled up and started making a lot of noise. We moved inside to our dining room. Everyone had a seat as I tried to broker an agreement about the girls and visitation, but no one was in the mood to compromise. The girls sat there, eyes wide open, watching the whole show. Things started to escalate, everyone talking at once, and I looked at Martha. I stood on my dining room chair, desperate to stop people from interrupting each other and yelled at the top of my lungs, "I think Martha has something to say."

She smiled at me and then bent down to reach into her bag. I felt better immediately. We had ammunition—what I expected her to pull out was the visitor log no one had ever signed. Instead, she pulled out her Bible and opened it to Psalm 1. I fought the urge to roll my eyes. These people did not share our faith. Everyone waited quietly—who was going to interrupt this senior with an open Bible? As she read, I could feel myself relaxing. She finished the passage about a tree planted by streams of water and looked up; she had changed the rhythm of the room.

She looked at me and then averted her eyes to the page, starting again, "*Salmos 2. Por que se amotinan las gentes . . .*"

(RVA). She read the rest of the chapter and without taking a breath, then moved into Psalm 3, 4, 5 . . .

We are in a spiritual filibuster! I giggled. *There are a lot of Psalms in this book. Eventually, we'll have to eat, go to the bathroom* . . . Psalm after Psalm, she continued to read until she was through chapter 10, culminating with verses 17-18, "You, LORD, hear the desire of the afflicted; you encourage them, and you listen to their cry, defending the fatherless and the oppressed, so that mere earthly mortals will never again strike terror." Lowering her reading glasses, Martha peered at our guests, "These girls don't belong to us any more than they do to you. They are daughters of the King Most High. Ask them where He has told them to live?"

The girls spoke their first and only word of the meeting. "Here," said one boldly, and "Here," followed the other.

The entourage stood up abruptly and moved to the door, speaking angry words in their departure at whoever was listening, threatening and swearing as they slipped into their car and roared off the campus.

I ran over to Martha, wanting to celebrate what felt like a victory! But her look stopped me cold. Sensing she had my attention, she grabbed her Bible, waved it in my face, now far more concerned about me than our departing guests. She said, "Don't you ever forget, *this* is the only sword you take into battle." I won't ever forget. Life lessons do that to you, they stick. This one reminds me it isn't ever what I bring to a table that saves the day. It's not my mouth, or contacts, or money, or position, or my whatever else I can fill the blank in with—it's God, and my pleas to Him, and the Word He's given me. And on any day, that's more than enough.

Martha and Barbara have a power I want—it's a power fueled by hope. Barbara prayed, hoping (which is different than wishing) in a Lord who was acting in a way she couldn't see. Martha stood strong, hoping (which is different than daring) in a God who has never let her down.

REFLECTION:

You, Lord, hear the desire of the afflicted; you encourage them, and you listen to their cry, defending the fatherless and the oppressed, so that mere earthly mortals will never again strike terror.
– PSALM 10:17-18

What does this truth tell you about yourself? Others? God?

CHANGE:

What battles are you facing? How do you fight?

ACTION:

Write down a verse that has meaning to you or write Psalm

10:17. Put it on your phone, in your pocket, or somewhere you'll see it throughout the day. When you are tempted to fight in your own strength, repeat it, asking God for strength and supernatural demonstrations of His power.

11

I Never Thought of Myself as a Priest

Yes to Second Chances

EXPERIENCE:

I was recently in a conversation with a youth pastor at one of the largest churches in the United States. He was sharing with me his journey, which included a divorce and a season of pain brought on by his own choices. Immediately following that period, he lost his prestigious ministry job and worked for several years in sales. Eventually, missing ministry, he put his resume on a Christian job board, willing to do anything. Then he heard from a large church.

He told me, "I was so surprised when they called. I was sure it was a joke. After everything that had unfolded in the last couple of years, I thought I would be lucky to get a volunteer position in ministry, let alone an interview at a church as reputable as this one."

"Were you honest?" I asked him, "Did you tell them what had happened?"

"It was all in my cover letter; they already knew when they called me. At the final interview, I asked the senior pastor what in particular led him to choose me for the position, knowing he had other, more qualified and less complicated choices." He shared that the pastor looked at him and said, "We have found in the church, most people have a season of brokenness. We like to look for staff on the other side of their broken season; it seems to make them better ministers of the gospel of grace." He shook his head as he recounted the whole scene to me, as if he still couldn't believe it. That's what happens when someone shows us a reckless kind of faith. It leaves us incredulous.

I practically leapt from my chair, "That's why your church is so big! More than creative programming or fancy speakers, if your pastor lives and loves like *that?* I don't know anyone who wouldn't want to be led by him."

Peter tells us, in 1 Peter 2:9, that we are God's priests. What is a priest's mission? A priest's chief responsibility is to show others what God is like. We can't *just* be recipients of His grace and goodness; we are also to be conduits or vessels of that goodness to others. All Christ-followers have a calling, and I don't mean the particulars of where we sense God asking us to be or serve. His larger mission is for us to put Him on display.

When someone interacts with a priest, a Christ-follower, they should know more about God after the exchange. This is true whether we are delivering good news or engaging in conflict. We need to conduct ourselves in such a way that, on the other side of our conversations, someone learns more about God's character. Maybe they understand His generosity, or His sensitivity, or His truth, or His grace, but whatever it is, it's the one task He has left us with: *represent Me through your actions to a lost world.*

That senior pastor demonstrated his full understanding of a redemptive gospel when he testified that God can use *all* things for His glory, even brokenness—especially brokenness. These days, I'm trying to be on the lookout and present enough in the moment to catch an opportunity to let the light inside me shine. It shines best through brokenness. This means, I sometimes need to bite my tongue when I want to share my opinion, and turn my watch around on my wrist so I won't be distracted by it. This means listening more, learning more, caring more . . . saying "yes" when "no" comes quicker to my tongue.

I can be tempted to put my best foot forward, but connection happens through vulnerability and whenever I humble myself before Jesus or those important to me—it's always His way. When I blow it with my kids, or my friends, or my husband, I can pretend like I didn't or, worse yet, I can pretend like it was their fault. But by pushing blame, all I do is create further chaos that needs to be cleaned up later. Instead, I should take responsibility and tell Jesus I want what He can give me. I want Him to use my confession to help me grow.

In our brokenness, God had mercy on us and extends grace each time we stumble. Like my friend who was extended a second chance at a new church, God extends second chances to us. In the trauma training Back2Back teaches, we talk about "redo's," the opportunity to give someone who has responded in their brokenness a second chance. Redo's have given me countless chances to say what I mean, to take a deep breath, to give the benefit of the doubt. God, in His mercy, gives us the ultimate redo, and He asks us to extend that same grace to others.

REFLECTION:

But this I call to mind, and therefore I have hope: The steadfast love of the Lord never ceases; his mercies never come to an end; they are new every morning; great is your faithfulness.
– LAMENTATIONS 3:21-23 (ESV)

But you are a chosen people, a royal priesthood, a holy nation, God's special possession, that you may declare the praises of him who called you out of darkness into his wonderful light.
– 1 PETER 2:9

What do these truths tell you about yourself? Others? God?

CHANGE:

How has your history and brokenness made you a better minister of the gospel of grace? How do you represent God to others?

ACTION:

Write a cover letter to someone as if you are applying for a job. What would you write to show the brokenness you have come through in your life?

12

It's Usually About Showing Up

Yes to Starting Somewhere

E X P E R I E N C E :

Naomi and I are painting our nails on the steps of the old chapel in her orphanage. It's our fourth coat of red. It is something we can do together without talking, and we like being together. I already know her favorite color (red) and her age (twelve). The only thing left in my Spanish repertoire is the Four Spiritual Laws. It's a hot, August afternoon, and we have nothing but time on our hands.

"Naomi," I start. She looks up from my nails, curious. "Do you know God loves you and has a wonderful plan for your life?" She shrugs her shoulders and gives me a look—part smirk, part annoyance, like she knows something I don't, and not the other way around. She was not receptive to the truth I was sharing with her. I go back to painting her nails and pray to God for another shot. Although completely true, in the face of her circumstances, she needs convincing.

Later that year, while hosting a team from the US, I try to explain why we invited them. "We need help with the children's hearts. There is nothing for the gospel to be planted in. We don't just need to cultivate the soil; we need to add soil, so the seed has someplace to take root." I look around and wonder if they understand what I'm saying. *Do they realize we have invited them here to paint fingernails?*

I grab a piece of paper. "Imagine this paper is the heart of an orphan. Each one has been abandoned or abused—no exceptions. For some, they don't remember the day they were dropped off; they just slowly grew up realizing they lived differently than the other children in school. For others, they do remember the moment they were left behind, and usually it starts with a lie. They are told they were going to a fair or a carnival, so they skipped off the bus or jumped out of the taxi and ran toward the other children. Not one of them would have gotten on the bus, if they had known they were going to an orphanage. Then, sometime later on that night, it hits them—they've been abandoned. Some of them are siblings. The oldest child feels responsible for their younger siblings; they wonder if their little brother or sister is eating or sleeping or doing well in school. On top of the weight of abandonment, the responsibility of being a caretaker for their siblings has been placed on their shoulders.

"Whenever that first moment of abuse or abandonment happens, it's like ripping a heart in half." I rip the paper. "Then, after that first rip, more start coming. You are the orphan kid in school [rip]. You aren't invited to someone's birthday party [rip]. You don't feel good and no one cares [rip]. It's your birthday and no one remembers [rip]. It's visitation day and no one comes to visit [rip]. It's visitation day and someone comes to visit you, but they only end up walking away [rip]. You don't play sports in school because there isn't anyone to pay the fees or pick you up [rip].

"Sometimes the rips happen because of the treatment you receive from other children or workers within the home [rip]. Sometime it comes from children at school who don't want to sit with you [rip]. Other rips come from punishments you receive that you didn't deserve [rip], or from words replaying in your mind, carelessly spoken [rip]. Sometimes it comes from adults who sense you are easy prey, and come back to hurt what is already considered damaged [rip].

"With each rip, the heart gets smaller and harder, so it's no wonder when I told Naomi, 'God loves you and has a wonderful plan for your life,' she gave me a look that said, 'Great plan. I don't want anything to do with a God who had *this* in mind.'"

Looking at the confetti of paper now strewn on the floor, I confess, "I wonder most days, 'What can we do? How can we possibly get started?'" My voice thick with emotion now, "I don't have the answer, but I do know it will take all of us. We have to start somewhere."

I meet their eyes. "Thanks for showing up. You'll spend this week picking up the pieces on the floor and depositing them back into the hearts of children." I pick up a piece of paper that has fallen on the ground. "Pushing their swing [deposit], remembering their name [deposit], sharing your Oreos [deposit], catching their frisbee [deposit]. Do it all not in your name, but in the name of Jesus. Eventually, the soil will be rich with deposits, enough for the gospel to take root." My hand is full of the ripped paper, and I hope the visual sticks in their minds.

There are millions of orphans in the world. Most people believe that half of the world's children have experienced trauma—that's one billion children. If I focus on the staggering numbers, I will never take any action. Instead, I simply ask myself how I can make a deposit in the life of one child today, and suddenly I feel creative, alive, and swept up into the movement of the Creator who is pursuing with a holy passion for "the least of these" (Matthew 25:40).

Todd and I are often asked, "How do you deal with so much heartbreak? Aren't you sad all the time?" The answer is complicated, and we all answer differently but, ultimately, we believe at some level *the story isn't over yet.* There is more to be written; it is a story full of hope and redemption. If I believed God was only loosely involved, passively observing as we make a mess of our lives, I would feel desperate about this state of affairs. But I believe in a God who is intricately woven into the soul of each person; He has written chapters we have yet to read and He picks up the pieces of our broken hearts. Most days, my role in the kingdom is as complicated as showing up and painting fingernails.

REFLECTION:

The Lord is not slow in keeping his promise, as some understand slowness. Instead he is patient with you, not wanting anyone to perish, but everyone to come to repentance.
— 2 PETER 3:9

What does this truth tell you about yourself? Others? God?

CHANGE:

Who have you sensed God ask you to practically make deposits into? Where are you showing up?

ACTION:

Get a piece of paper and rip it, remembering how you've

been torn apart. Grieve with the Lord over your brokenness. Then pick up the pieces and thank Him for the people who have made deposits of healing in your life. Reach out and thank them for how they've encouraged you.

13

Now God Has
My Attention
Yes to Growing

It is March and we're spending the weekend traveling to Texas, enjoying some family fellowship and Texas hospitality. It should have been the perfect weekend, but as I walk along San Antonio's famed Riverwalk, all I can think is *where is the closest bathroom?* I've been battling a stomach flu for a week now, and I'm getting tired of it. A month later, while at the Easter service at church, I have to leave in the middle because my stomach is upset again.

May and June are a blur. We eventually ask the doctors why I can't keep food down anymore. I've never been sick as an adult; I have never even had allergies. By July, the doctors have a diagnosis: gastroparesis, a condition in which your food doesn't digest, so after an extended time in your stomach, it has to come back up. The problem is, there's no reason for me to have developed this condition. Most people who have it are diabetic, have had intestinal surgery, or have some sort of tumor or blockage. Also, the doctors add, "this condition usually gets progressively worse and has no cure."

On the last day of July, José Angel, a pastor friend of ours, came to our house. Although he has an appearance that looks like he forgot to get ready that morning, he has a heart of pure gold. I have trouble admitting weakness and I don't like to ask people for help. Pastor José Angel is not one of my most intimate friends, so I haven't told him about the extent of my illness. All he knows is that I haven't been coming around where he has his ministry—which makes his following comment to me even more amazing.

"Beth, I had a dream last week, and I'm sorry it has taken this long to tell you about it. I know you've been sick, but I want you to know God has healed you." My conservative roots kick in, and I lift an eyebrow in skepticism. José Angel continues, "In my dream, there was a demon wrapped around your stomach, but it has now been released. God has allowed it for a season, so when you encounter demonic forces in the future, you'll recognize them and how they move. He wants to use you to free others.

But today you are free, so go and walk in your healing." He finishes and smiles.

Never before have I experienced anything like that. Not one thing in his entire story seems believable to me. Still, I let him pray over me, but I feel no "tingling" of miraculous healing. I walk back to the house, immediately get sick, and feel frustrated. Late one night, two days later, my friend Sonia, who's married to another pastor here in Mexico, calls me on the phone. She sounds anxious, "Beth, I just had this dream about you and had to call and tell you about it . . ." and she proceeds to describe the same dream Pastor José Angel had—same message, same promise of healing. The odd thing is, Pastor José Angel and Sonia don't even know each other.

Now God has my attention.

I scheduled a trip home to Ohio the next week, where I planned to see a medical specialist to pursue further treatment. I wrestle with what to tell him. I'm not even sure what to think myself. In his office, I say, "Here's my file, here are my tests, here's my health history—and here's my frustration with the last couple of months." I probably tell him far more than he needs to know. He nods, looks over the files, and eventually concludes, "You're very sick."

I look away. *Should I tell him about the dreams?*

I dive in. "Here's the thing, for the past week, I have been feeling better. Not all-at-once or anything, but a little better every day. I've been eating some, and it's been staying down. I don't know how you feel about this—I don't really know how I feel about it—but I think a demon may have been released, and I am healed."

"Wow." He pauses. "Normally, since these tests are less than a month old, I would use them to determine my treatment plan, but let's repeat them and see where we stand." That seems logical and safe. I like what I can read on a chart. I repeat the myriad of tests.

Days later, the specialist calls me. "Beth, in my left hand are the test results you brought from Mexico showing me you are very sick. But in my right hand are the tests you took a few days ago telling me you are healthy. I propose no ongoing medical treatment for you at this time." He pauses, then adds, "And yes, I do think it's a miracle."

I don't understand it, but I need to testify to it. Do I think a demon had his "hand" around my stomach? I don't know, but it sure felt like it. My faith grew throughout this process. It grew when I let José pray over me. It grew again when I let Sonia pray over me. It grew when I boldly told the doctor in Ohio about my friends' dreams. And it grew as I heard the new results and rejoiced in the miraculous healing.

If faith could fit in a frame, the way a painting does, then we might get tired of looking at it after a couple of years. But faith, as it grows, keeps demanding a new and larger frame to be housed in. I think the Lord loves to do things that are unexpected, things beyond what we can control or predict. It forces our canvas of faith to get bigger. God consistently breaks the boundaries (my frame) with which I've surrounded Him. Enlarging the frame of my faith means admitting my finiteness and rigidity. It means He is dangerously greater than I can define or even understand. I am different now: I minister differently, I pray differently, I look for new aspects of His character. I no longer say "never" because I have had an up-close-and-personal encounter with a demon. I now think literally anything is possible. People can reconcile, bodies can heal, doors can open. I don't know why or how or when, but I know we can hope and I know we can believe. I also know we are opposed, and there is a whole world of warfare we only understand in part.

Some people would look at José Angel and think about all the ways they could "teach and train" him. But I'm not sure I can ever match what he offered to me. He and Sonia were listening to the Lord so intently that they caught a message meant for me. Then they trusted in the Spirit that led them to share what must have been uncomfortable. And their act of faith helped heal me and increased my own faith.

There is no way to train someone to have that kind of faith. Pastor José Angel's and Sonia's faith is a humble, quiet sort of faith—a faith which is unbelievably reckless.

REFLECTION:

"But I will restore you to health and heal your wounds,"
declares the LORD.
– JEREMIAH 30:17

What does this truth tell you about yourself? Others? God?

CHANGE:

What has forced your canvas to get bigger? Do you believe
in miracles?

ACTION:

Find a picture (either personal or online) that represents
something miraculous to you. Could be a baby or something in nature, could be the face of someone who has been
healed. Frame it and place it somewhere it will serve as a
reminder that God still moves.

14

Less Duty,
More Pep Rally

Yes to Giving

I pulled into a field, unsure of what to expect. I was worshipping on this Sunday with an ECWA congregation, the Evangelical Church of West Africa. Upon entering the rough-cut, one-room sanctuary building, I was delightfully met with the sounds, sights, and smells of Africa.

You never know when you sit down in church what piece of the service will stir you. Sometimes it's a beautiful moment in worship, sometimes it's a stirring point in the message, other times it's the quiet reflection in prayer, or a meaningful communion table. This day, it was the offering.

And I am pretty sure, for me, that was a first.

It started out as a beautiful song about a widow. Her life now required hard work to keep the family together. The lyrics lamented in a minor key about the role she must play as both mother and father, and the little relief she will now experience here on earth. The group was singing in a combination of English and Hausa, but there was enough of my language for me to be able to enjoy both the rhythm and the words.

Then a woman moved down the aisle and, as if performing a skit, danced around the altar, using a broom to pretend to sweep the floor. Eventually, she switched to a field tool as she "harvested," all the while never standing straight up, always bent over, emphasizing her backbreaking responsibilities. While she worked, we sang a chorus about this hardworking widow, who relies on and draws comfort from her audience of One.

Next, the notes moved out of minor keys, and there was a shift in the melody as the rhythm beat faster, almost to a chant. People sang louder as the words now addressed the church, those of us who were watching the widow. We were suddenly a part of the scene—the skit essentially widening, with all of us now playing the part of the village, watching her work. I could feel compassion rising, as the noise became deafening. I wanted to reach out to her, to help her with the broom, to straighten her back, to pray with her, and encourage her. *What must that feel like, constant fear she won't have enough for her children now?*

As if on a cue they all knew (even though I didn't), the aisles filled with the women of the church, carrying on their heads bags of corn, rice, beans, or handfuls of *naira* (the Nigerian currency), and they laid them down at the feet of this widow. It was akin to a special offering a church might make for a natural disaster or a visiting missionary, something above and beyond; although it was unlike anything I had ever seen. Technically, it was an offering, but it was way more than that—a combination of celebration, responsibility, and privilege all wrapped up in one.

Deuteronomy 24:19-22 records God's commands to the Israelites regarding the harvest:

> *When you are harvesting in your field and you overlook a sheaf, do not go back to get it. Leave it for the foreigner, the fatherless and the widow, so that the Lord your God may bless you in all the work of your hands. When you beat the olives from your trees, do not go over the branches a second time. Leave what remains for the foreigner, the fatherless and the widow. When you harvest the grapes in your vineyard, do not go over the vines again. Leave what remains for the foreigner, the fatherless and the widow. Remember that you were slaves in Egypt. That is why I command you to do this.*

This congregation was obeying these verses from Deuteronomy, but it felt less like a duty and more like a pep rally. My mind couldn't help but flash to the offering box fixed to the wall outside of the sanctuary in churches I have attended and admired. So many of our churches today don't even include an offering as a part of the worship service anymore, lest we offend someone. We have taken pride in the fact we aren't asking for money in the American church, so people can come and not suspect an ulterior motive, but are we missing out on this beautiful dance, this joyful release of our first fruits in obedience? The fulfillment each woman was experiencing as she handed over a part of her own hard work was contagious—it was worship. What a contrast to the scene in millions of churches that morning across the globe. Churches like ones I have sat in and, more than once, been guilty of reaching in my wallet and releasing what I thought was the bare minimum I had to give, to keep my holiness intact.

I so wanted to join in the dance; I wanted to help that widow. I wanted to loosen my grip on what I had earned on behalf of those He has asked us to care for. I sat for a moment in my pew, sweating in the African heat, moving with a rhythm you don't hear as much as feel, and debating my next move. Grabbing some *naira* from my backpack and feeling both sheepish and compelled, I sashayed my way down the aisle, closed my eyes, and released what can never satisfy, to worship.

I spent days afterwards thinking about that offering. *What do I give to God? Do I do so reluctantly, begrudgingly? Is it enough?* God doesn't need my money, He just knows what happens to me when I am generous, and invites me into that goodness. *Do I delight in and rush to give what I have been given right back?* I am grateful God's Holy Spirit flashlight shined on this in my heart. There was some cleaning up to do with my attitude. If I am not careful, I can slip easily into an "earn and deserve" mentality, when God has invited me into something so much more. I don't dance my way today to an offering box in Ohio, it would draw unnecessary attention, but I am trying to celebrate every time I release what was always His back into His hand.

REFLECTION:

When you are harvesting in your field and you overlook a sheaf, do not go back to get it. Leave it for the foreigner, the fatherless and the widow, so that the Lord your God may bless you in all the work of your hands. When you beat the olives from your trees, do not go over the branches a second time. Leave what remains for the foreigner, the fatherless and the widow. When you harvest the grapes in your vineyard, do not go over the vines again. Leave what remains for the foreigner, the fatherless and the widow. Remember that you were slaves in Egypt. That is why I command you to do this.
– DEUTERONOMY 24:19-22

What does this tell you about yourself? Others? God?

CHANGE:

What does tithing feel like to you? What has been hard to let go of that you've offered in worship to God?

ACTION:

Look at your finances and evaluate your tithes and offerings. How are you doing with releasing back to God what is already His? Decide to align your practices with your convictions.

15

One Missed Shot

Yes to Trying Again

My involvement in sports started sometime around fifth grade and continued throughout high school. Despite my best hopes, genetics would determine I stop growing in the ninth grade, so my 5'4" frame wasn't getting a lot of action under anyone's basketball hoop. I learned if I wanted to ever play basketball and, more importantly, contribute, I needed to learn to develop an outside shot. For many years, I worked on my arc and accuracy until I could be the player people would pass to on the top of the key.

During a Christmas basketball tournament in high school, our team kept winning until eventually we earned a spot in the final game. We played evenly against our competition throughout the entire four quarters and found our-selves down by one, with less than thirty seconds left on the game clock. Coach Kiehl called a time-out and looked at me. "Do you think if we get you the ball, you could pop one up from the outside before they have a chance to organize much of a defense? You think you can make it?"

I looked around the huddle at my teammates and said, more confidently than I felt, "Yes, get it to me. I'll do it."

My friend Dawn dribbled down the court and passed me the ball. I squared up, eyed the backboard, and threw up the shot. It ringed around the rim . . . and then rolled out. Seconds later, the buzzer went off and the game was over. We lost the tournament by one point.

I don't remember much about the after-game speech our coach gave; what I most remember was not wanting to face the parents of my friends, who I knew would offer me looks of frustration, or pity, or some combination. I took my time gathering my things in the locker room and finally, when I was sure everyone was gone, I made my way out to see my dad, who was waiting to take me home. As I walked through the double doors to the gym, I saw my dad with a ball under his arm. He didn't say anything, just looked at me and passed me the ball, pointing on the floor to where I had missed the shot. I caught the ball, and—hurt—I squared up and shot. *Swish.* I rolled my eyes and held up two fingers, then reached down for my bag. I gave him the sarcastic look teenage girls have long perfected, *Satisfied?* He rebounded my ball, ignored my look, and passed me the ball again, pointing back to the floor, telling me where I needed to shoot. I threw the ball up with less accuracy and still made it. Catching the ball, he passed it to me a third time. *Swish.* This went on for another few baskets until my quivering lip finally gave way to the tears that had been hovering. He rebounded the last ball and walked over to bear hug me.

"What is it you want?" I said, angry.

He pulled back to look me in the eye, hoping his teachable moment would land in my heart, "I just wanted you to go to bed tonight remembering what it is you are *capable* of."

Dads have a way of saying things that just stick with you. I heard him loud and clear that night: One set back does not make me a failure. One missed shot is just that, *one missed shot.* My dad taught me that night to remember what I am capable of in the face of failure; he was desperate to make sure I would be ready to try again.

Sometimes we fall short of our standards and expectations for ourselves. Lies and insecurities come rushing in. We forget that God has called us, equipped us, given us promises, given us gifts. We forget what we are capable of. In these moments, it is important to listen to the voice of God and to the people around you who love you. They say, "You are capable. You are gifted. You are loved. You are not your mistakes, you are not your missed shots or your failed attempts." The voices from the peanut gallery that sound condemning and shame-based either don't have freedom themselves or don't usually find themselves with the ball at the last minute in the game. We can't give their voices or the inner critic in us more power than the Truth as God speaks it. He has given us a purpose and a path that is sure. Even though we might stumble, our future is always secure in Him. He is always there to remind us what we are capable of; all we have to do is say *yes* to trying again.

REFLECTION:

A highway will be there, a roadway, And it will be called the Highway of Holiness The unclean will not travel on it, But it will be for him who walks that way, And fools will not wander on it.
– ISAIAH 35:8 (NASB)

What does this truth tell you about yourself? Others? God?

CHANGE:

What have you forgotten you are capable of? Whose voice in your life cheers you on?

ACTION:

Write down ten strengths God has given you and say a prayer of thanksgiving for them. Think about how God might be able to use your strengths to fulfill the purpose He has for your life.

16

Green Pastures

Yes to Trusting

When I was seventeen, my dad and I went on a daddy-daughter date in his Mustang convertible toward what was then farming country. We ate Dilly Bars and breezed past the white picket fences. My dad points out the fences that are bowed outward toward the road. "Look how silly those cows are," he says. "They lean against the fences, not realizing they could break through, fall onto the road, and be killed. They want to walk up the road and find other fields when they have their own green pastures they can romp through."

More fences pass by.

"I read somewhere that a cow's brain is the size of a human fist," I add helpfully. "Those cows sure are dumb . . ." We ride a little while longer when my dad shifts in his seat and says, "Beth, you are like the cow. The Lord has provided you with so many green pastures to find satisfaction in, and I feel like all you do is press against the fence. Don't you realize if you break through, there's danger on the other side?"

I brace myself, preparing for the typical teenage lecture about things that are dangerous and harmful. I was totally prepared to tune him out. However, he never mentions the dangerous road again, instead he spends the rest of our time talking about how rich God's pastures are for him. How he has found life, adventure, meaning, and purpose in the pasture God has provided for him. That's all I wanted, I just thought it was on the other side of whatever fence I found myself against. But I trust my heavenly Father and my earthly father, and if they say goodness is in my pasture, I will believe them.

Listening to my dad talk about his relationship with Christ made faith unbelievably attractive to me that day; it made faith seem like a relationship, not an exercise. I learned the benefit of the pasture is greater than the attraction of the road.

. . .

I am reminded of this lesson my dad taught me as I look after Maria. Maria is a young girl who was born with a chip on her shoulder. That chip was put there by the father she never knew, by the mother who preferred her own pursuit of religious activities to her daughter, and by everyone who turned a blind eye to her abusive stepfather. All that dysfunction paved Maria's road to the orphanage, and by the time I met her, she had a beautiful smile, a bright mind, and an elephant-sized attitude problem. Her attitude made her living at the children's home an impossibility, as the workers and other girls couldn't manage her behavior any longer. Convinced all she needed was love, I invited her to live with me and my family.

One night, while on a date with Todd, I got a sense something was wrong at home. A beep on my "mom radar," Todd calls it.

"Just call home and check it out," he encouraged me.

"*Bueno*. Hey, it's me. Is Maria home yet from her English class?" I asked my daughter who answers the phone. *I am sure she's fine*, I think, as she searches the house.

"No, she isn't back yet from class," came back the answer. "Wasn't she supposed to be home hours ago?"

Yes, she was. Ok, now I am concerned. "We'll head home, but if you hear from her first, call me back, will you?"

We set out to look for Maria on our way home. At this point, we are more worried something has happened *to* her than *because* of her, and we make calls to her friends and pray as we drive between school and home. I'm a cup-half-full person, usually quick to give the benefit of the doubt, looking for the silver lining—all the time believing Maria hasn't done something she knows she shouldn't. Todd and I began to fight a little, him concluding much faster than me that wherever Maria is, she *wants* to be there.

Later that night we found her—in the backseat of an old car with a man twice her age. I was crushed. Not long after that, Maria left us, unable to live within the boundaries we set for our home. I didn't hear from her for several months. Then, one night, she shows up bleeding and barely clothed. She had walked—barefoot—all the way down the unpaved road to our home. Someone saw her coming from far off and ran to get me. As I approach her, she calmly explains that she had been hit with a cement block by her angry pimp. I clean up what should have been painful abrasions, and I'm struck by the fact she doesn't flinch; she doesn't seem to feel any pain at all.

"Doesn't this hurt?" I asked.

"Not really."

I'm amazed how still she sits as I treat her cuts and bruises, "How can this not hurt? These are rocks in your face!"

"I don't feel anything physical anymore," she said. "I haven't for a while." After her first few "tricks," she explained, she stopped feeling anything when someone touched her.

Maria loves the other side of the fence, the feeling no one is controlling her. She loves the road more than the pasture. She has been on that road so long now, she strolls down the middle, not even dodging when she hears a car coming. To warn her about the dangers of that sort of life is pointless now. What she needs is to believe there is the peace and comfort and love offered back in the green pastures, unconditionally.

I still see Maria from time to time. She reaches out to let me know where she is and how she's doing. She isn't ready to come off the road, but she has a gnawing curiosity about whether I still like it over here in the pasture. Living my life on purpose—with joy and adventure, love and risk—is the best ministry plan I have. It's exactly what Jesus had in mind when he said in Matthew 5:14, "You are the light of the world . . ." The Bible teaches us we are a part of the kingdom of priests, which means I represent the God I love and serve. When Maria spends time with me, she's supposed to get an impression on how God is. That thought stops me from judging her, or rejecting her (which is more natural for me to do). It creates spiritual space inside of me that I can ask God to fill. *What does she need?* I don't know, but He does, and I want to be a willing vessel for Him to use. I don't know when Maria will walk through my door again, ready to leave the road, or if it will even be my door she walks through. But in the meantime, my goal is to make sure she sees me enjoying the pastures whenever she sneaks a look.

Over and over again, God teaches me that for those

with reckless faith the story is *never* over. It's childish to throw in the towel, pout, get frustrated, or walk away. Life isn't a puzzle that's too hard or a toy you can't figure out. Trying circumstances aren't excuses to give up on people. But so often, I'm tempted to lose faith when I'm confronted with a setback or a broken heart over people or circumstances. When I relax my control on the plotline of my life and give in to the journey God has prepared for me, I lose myself in all the great stories swirling around me. When I stomp my feet and say, "That's not fair!" or "It wasn't supposed to happen that way!" then I run out of gas, and my spiritual journey stalls.

God is teaching me, one child at a time, one friend at a time, one day at a time . . . He is the Author of life and can redeem and write any story He wants, in His timing, however He chooses. It's my job not to control, worry, manipulate, or fuss. It's my job to say *yes*, trust, and enjoy the pastures that God has placed me in.

REFLECTION:

He makes me lie down in green pastures, he leads me beside quiet waters, he refreshes my soul. He guides me along the right paths for his name's sake.
– PSALM 23:2-3

What does this truth tell you about yourself? Others? God?

CHANGE:

What story are you in right now you are believing isn't over
yet? Where do you lean on the fence?

ACTION:

Thank God for the green pastures in your life. Take a drink
of really cold water and feel how refreshing it feels. Tell the
Lord you want only His living water to refill you when you
are depleted, and to spill out of you onto others.

17

What Kind of Meat
Does God Bring?

Yes to Mountains Moving

Once, after I spoke in an Ohio church, someone came up and asked if I was talking about Monterrey, Mexico in my sermon, because he traveled there for work and he would like to visit where we serve. We exchanged business cards and I remembered his name was Carlos, but I lost his card immediately. He didn't lose mine and, four months later, he called and we arranged to meet at dinnertime after his work day.

"Who was that?" Todd asked as I hung up the phone.

"Some guy named Carlos, I met him in Cincinnati.

We are going to eat dinner with him tonight and show him around," I answered.

Todd's questions began: "What's his last name? Who does he work for? What's he doing in town?" I shrug my shoulders and offer up hopefully, "I met him in a church; I am sure he's harmless."

"First let me go down to where he's working, and I will check it out." Todd insisted and, hours later, ventured downtown to meet him.

. . .

Meanwhile, at a children's home in the area, the director, Edgar, was awake this same Saturday morning wondering where the children's second meal of the day would come from. Had Edgar picked up the phone and called us, we would have brought over beans, rice, eggs, oil, and tortillas—that's why we lived in the city, to provide food to orphan children! We would have been happy to provide inexpensive food we could get in large quantities, enough to sustain them until we could get something more significant. But Edgar was afraid the children were putting us in a place only Jesus belonged (as the Giver of all good gifts). So, Edgar prays silently for future provision, and feeds the fifty children a brunch meal, using the last of his *pesos*.

Later, when the children were expecting their supper, Edgar calls them to the dining room. "We don't have any food for tonight's dinner. But we know for sure God hears us when we pray, and you are some of his most favorite children. Let's pray and ask him to bring our dinner."

They started to pray, and almost immediately Edgar is interrupted by Joel, one of the youngest boys, *"Tío,* we're praying God brings us dinner?" says Joel slowly, "What kind of food does *God* bring?"

Edgar, looking for a teachable moment, seizes this chance, "Joel, God loves you, and you are His child. He wants you to know He sees you. Let's see what He will deliver."

They prayed again.

Joel interrupted a second time, *"Tío,* do you think . . . God will bring us . . . *meat?"*

To a little boy whose diet is mainly beans, rice, tortillas, and eggs, meat seems like a big request.

They bowed their heads again, praying for dinner and meat in Jesus' name, until Joel couldn't stand it any longer. He asked (in the way preschoolers continue on with their questioning), *"Tío,* what *kind* of meat does God bring? I bet if He's God, He brings steak."

. . .

Todd calls me, "Beth, your friend Carlos isn't allowed to take his product back over the border and he is just going to throw all of it out, but I assured him we could use it. He's talking the other vendors into donating to us as well. Forget meeting us for dinner; I am going to start dropping it off at the children's homes right now. Can you call ahead and let them know I am coming?"

Joel and Edgar's home is first on his route. When I call ahead to let Edgar know that Todd is on his way with food, Edgar doesn't seem surprised.

"What's he bringing over?" he asked.

"I don't know, Todd just wanted me to make sure you had room in your freezer."

"I have some room in my freezer," Edgar said.

"Great, he'll be there in about ten minutes," I prepare to hang up.

"Beth, do you know what's going *in* the freezer?"

I fought for patience, "He's at some meat convention downtown, so I am betting it's meat."

"Beth . . . would you mind terribly finding out exactly what kind of meat it is?" he asked hesitantly.

"What do you mean, 'What kind of meat?' It's meat, Edgar. It's food. Why should it matter?"

"Just, would you mind calling me back when you know?"

I dial Todd and asked, "What *kind* of meat is it? Edgar wants to know."

Todd replied, "Beth, you won't believe it. It's the best meat money can buy—incredible cuts of steak—they are trying to attract some new restaurant business in the city. It's filet mignon, New York strip, T-bone, sirloin. They're going to love it."

I called Edgar back to report.

"Praise God!" he then asks me to hold as he shouts out to the children, "God's on His way over with your steak!"

Jesus talked in Matthew 17 about how faith isn't measured by the one it dwells in. Regardless of the size of someone's faith, if it's true, then it's effective and can activate change, even move a mountain. Those children prayed with the faith of a mustard seed, and the mountain moved. And it's still moving.

I've told Joel many times that God has big plans for his life. To teach a preschooler his prayers are heard, and that those prayers move the same hand of God that created the mountains Joel looks at every day, is a mighty heady lesson for a four-year-old. It's a big lesson for me as well. I often don't see God provide meat in my life because I already have a plan in place to secure it, and, more often than not, it doesn't involve consulting the Lord. Had Edgar relied on humans that day to provide for his children, rather than wait on God, he would most likely have received beans and rice and eggs and tortillas. There's nothing wrong with eating that, and the children would have been grateful, but there is something otherworldly about a King who provides banquet food for His children.

How often do I settle for beans when, if I had only waited on God, I might have been given steak?

REFLECTION:

And God is able to bless you abundantly, so that in all things at all times, having all that you need, you will abound in every good work.
– 2 CORINTHIANS 9:8

What does this truth tell you about yourself? Others? The Lord?

CHANGE:

When do you cry out to man instead of God? What have you asked God for? When does our helping get in the way of God's work?

ACTION:

Gather some friends and buy groceries or make a meal for someone you think might benefit from extra help this week.

18

Making It Better

Yes to the Extraordinary Rescue Plan

Several years ago, when my family and I were living in Ohio, my children asked me if we could take their friends on a trip to Monterrey, so they could show their friends where they grew up. That year, we traveled with sixty students and have every year since. This year on the trip, we took all the children in a children's home in Monterrey to a bowling alley. It was a fantastic activity for about 90 percent of the group. But there were a couple of children, because of age, or attention, or disability, who played on the fringe.

I kept circling the group like a sheep dog, making sure

the Fanta spills were getting cleaned up and the bathroom breaks weren't taking too long. I applauded the strikes and spares and took pictures of new friendships forming. One of the mission trip guests had traveled to Mexico with a broken heart, and because few of us were privy to the challenging circumstances of his life, no one knew how to make it better. He was outside the group activity, emulating what I was doing by attending to those not fully engaged.

Then a little girl too young to sustain a game of bowling snuck up and pulled on his hand, running away once she had his attention. When he spun around and locked eyes with her, his whole face lit up and the making-it-better began. They spent the rest of the afternoon engaged in chase, hide and seek, and good snacking. This little girl was seen, not as a nuisance, but as a child. He was seen, not for his problems, but for his person. I watched the American boy's face relax over the course of the afternoon. I wondered who that day was the real "missionary"? Might God have been using the girl to lift the boy's spirit? To bring good gifts of joy and connection and relief?

There are dozens of promises God has written specifically for the orphan, and I spent the first season of my missionary journey thinking it was my job to put flesh on those promises in order to represent Him. And while that's good thinking, it's not complete. Time + challenge + spiritual discipline = maturation, and with growing maturation came the stark realization this is not an "us" and "them" situation. I am every bit a spiritual orphan as the children we serve. I need those promises as much as they do. I need to be spiritually rescued as much as they do. I can easily have an "orphan spirit" and forget my identity in Christ and all that comes with it. I can have hard circumstances or hurt feelings overwhelm me. When I do, I need rescued, lifted up, heard, and extended mercy. God cares about me, and has adopted me into His family—literally grafted me in. The written promises in the Bible are now reminders to His children of how He has a plan for us, how He is making it all better.

I am just more convinced than ever that God is multi-faceted. He cares about the heart of the child sponsor, as much as He does the little girl she sponsors. He comes through for the needs of children around the world and He comes through for us. When I realized God loved the giver, the goer, and the one to whom we serve all the same, it felt like my eyes opened. I now see God's work going on all around me. It's the way people love and listen and treat each other. It's the overflow of what's happening between us and God.

God started this great work of His in the Garden of Eden—He made His people, He put them in His presence, they were in His place, and experiencing His complete peace. One day, Revelations 21 promises, we will again be in His place, experiencing His presence, and feeling His peace. As author Sandra L. Richter says in her book *The Epic of Eden*, "Everything in-between is this extraordinary rescue plan," and we are invited into it! You, me, the orphan . . . we are all broken, with an outstanding invitation to be grafted into God's family and express His heart as passionately as we can. That's how making-it-better works.

REFLECTION:

> *I have said these things to you, that in me you may have peace.*
> *In the world you will have tribulation. But take heart;*
> *I have overcome the world.*
> – JOHN 16:33 (ESV)

What does this truth tell you about yourself? Others? God?

CHANGE:

Have you ever seen yourself as a spiritual orphan? How do you see God's extraordinary rescue plan playing out around you?

ACTION:

Write the list of promises God gives to orphans and imagine God saying them directly to you. Which one jumps out at you? What promise do you need to cling to and stand on today?

19

Never Bored

Yes to Dynamic

EXPERIENCE:

When I was about six years old, I remember my mom threatening to wash my mouth out with soap—not because I'd said a bad word or because I was sassy to my mother. I had simply said the one word that can still make her wild: *bored*. On rainy days, or summer evenings, or during long programs designed for adults, I was not allowed to say, "This is boring" or "I'm bored." If my mom even thought she smelled those words coming, she would quietly remind me that my attitude was what I made of it. If I was bored, it was because I was boring.

There were easily a thousand things she could (and would) name I could do. She was on a mission to ensure we not see life (or her) as a source of entertainment. Life was what we made of it. Although I've since teased her about all this, she was right. This principle relates to our relationship with God as well. If God bores us, it is we who are boring. He came to give us life to the full. He is infinite and wild. He is fascinating and crying out for us to participate in a life He has designed specifically for us. Will we fashion Him into something He is not so that we can more easily understand or explain Him? Or will we let Him be what we can't understand, but are still drawn to?

I still need to be reminded of the fundamental lesson that God's ways are nothing like mine. He is consistent but hardly predictable. You can pray for healing for four people, and only one might get better. For every story of a Joel getting steak, hundreds of people die of hunger. When someone dies, despite our prayers for their healing, or when something we pray for doesn't happen, we tend to believe God doesn't always come through. We get good at explaining to children and new believers why bad things happen to good people, why there's evil in the world, and why "our guy" doesn't always win. But I'm slowly learning to refuse to be tripped up by such things. When troubles approach, I used to always plan an escape route, thinking that it would keep both God and me from looking bad. But He doesn't require any such excuses.

That night with Joel was a turning point in my faith. I was headed down a path where I believed God and I were working together to meet the needs of abandoned children, as if we were equal partners in His grand plan. I knew how to ask what needs people had, and I had learned how to ask those who had resources to help meet those needs—and there were lots of days when I could neatly draw a line between the two and fall into bed with a sense of self-righteousness—*God and I are quite the team.* But I'm learning to let my back get pushed against a wall—because that is when I cry out for my Rescuer. Most days when I see the wall coming, I angle myself so I don't get anywhere near it. I decide not to say something I should, or not to take a risk I've been dying to take. I'm slowly learning to get in over my head, so God can save the day—or at least pick up the pieces. I want to take risks so I can't bail myself out, so I am even more grateful when God shows up. Sometimes He not only shows up, but He shows off.

The more childlike and less refined my faith becomes, the easier it is to invite God to come. Never again will I offer up an explanation that spins God as weak or passive. If God doesn't come through in the way I want Him to, it should expand my view of faith, not shrink it. It means there is something else going on, something I can't see or understand, and I have the opportunity to be swept up in it. I am walking toward a more reckless faith. It is not defined by my denomination; its doctrine is constantly in flux as my understanding of how He moves in this world grows. Some days, my faith even feels downright dangerous. *Am I allowed to think that about God? Can I ask that of Him?* I think He is more fascinated with our dialogue than He is disapproving of my missteps.

But my relationship with God feels dynamic, and I believe He wants to be the place I come with my delight *and* fear, my questions *and* gratitude. Dynamic is the opposite of static, and static is the death of a relationship. May our *yes* continue to put us in a posture of worship and wonder.

REFLECTION:

The LORD does whatever pleases him, in the heavens and on the earth, in the seas and all their depths.
– PSALM 135:6

What does this truth tell you about yourself? Others? The Lord?

CHANGE:

When have you made excuses for God? When have you felt spiritually in over your head?

ACTION:

Plan a day to fast and use that time to cry out to God for your needs. Be reminded that Jesus sustains us and is the Bread of Life. Write down any new thoughts that come to you this day about the circumstances you lifted up to Him.

20

The Beginning of a Much Larger Adventure

Yes to Childlike Faith

"Why are they so scantily clad?" I ask. I'm sixteen years old, on my first mission trip, and we have just arrived at a refugee camp on the border between Costa Rica and Nicaragua. One of the hosts says, "Well, they've just walked over eighty miles through the wilderness. Most of them have used their clothes to burn, bury the dead, trap animals, eat . . ." Another volunteer impatiently asks me, "Why? Does it bother you?"

Yes, it does bother me, but I'm not offended by their appearance. Rather, I'm saddened and moved by it. I spend that day alternating between dispersing used clothing and performing a drama our team has prepared—all of which creates a wave of conflicting feelings in me. I wonder whether the clothing or the drama matter more to God. In the back of my mind, I picture my own amply-filled closet, and I feel confused. On our last day at the camp, I don't want to leave. I need to know how I can keep helping, even after our group has left. I march up to the busy director and ask him breathlessly, "My name is Beth, and tomorrow I go back to my hometown, what can I do? What are your needs?"

"We need clothes and food," he says and then walks away. I think now I would recognize this as a brush off, but I left feeling commissioned.

That fall, with my prepared slide show, flyers, and thoughts, I go to area high schools, promising if they give up their used clothing, we will deliver it to those who need it most. I then arrange with a local amusement park to use their passenger pick-up area, where, months later, I stand and wait as people come by to drop off their boxes.

"Dad, look at all these boxes!" I practically squeal with excitement later that day. My father has taken off work to be with me. A man pulls up to unload his bags from the trunk of his Monte Carlo.

"Hey," he says, pulling out his wallet, "are you taking cash donations for the shipping?"

I just stand there, stunned. *Shipping?* I'd never thought

of that detail. In all my weeks of planning, it never occurred to me I'd need to pay to have all these clothes shipped. He waits for a response, and I have none. After all the promises I've made, I wonder if I can really keep them. My dad comes up behind me, "There's been a private donation given to cover the shipping expenses." Satisfied, the man shrugs and puts his five dollars back in his pocket. I look at my dad. Without even asking, I know he and my mom are the ones making this "private donation."

The journey I am on today started back then, on the day I delivered those packages in several trips to the post office. At sixteen, I wasn't thinking strategically. Not until years later did it occur to me how ridiculous it was to write such a large check to a shipping company to send old shoes to Latin America. It would have been wiser to write that same check to an organization in-country, where the money could have purchased three times the amount of used clothing.

But, of course, that's not the point. That day my dad and I were both following the prompting of the Holy Spirit in our hearts, and we obeyed. I now see that this prompting of the Holy Spirit and my obedience was the spark to a much larger adventure. Though it might not have made sense to my dad to spend his money that way, following God's will doesn't always look logical. It can sometimes look downright reckless. We need to use our brains and follow what's considered wisdom, but we also need to be sensitive to the Holy Spirit and understand that discernment is more valuable than logic. My dad wasn't just paying to ship old clothes overseas; his check was really seed money for something that took root in my heart. Now, whenever I find myself only making decisions based on "what makes sense," I stop and ask the Lord if I'm missing something. *Is there another decision that involves something I don't necessarily understand but should be willing to obey?*

The year before I moved to Mexico and the "missionary" events of my life unfolded, my Dad died of cancer. On this side of eternity, he may have wondered whether his contribution to my clothing fund was really a smart decision, but from his perspective now, as a member of that great cloud of witnesses, he knows such investments, directed by the Lord, pay off in ways not humanly conceivable.

How easy it is for me to make my faith look "refined." Under the guise of good stewardship, I can plan and plot my way toward responsible living. I'm a mother and I have a savings account, I have insurance, and most days I drive the speed limit. I take vitamins and don't carry credit card debt. Responsible living is a good thing, but does it always need to look so refined? Can't we throw caution to the wind from time to time—and spend money on a used clothing project—not because it makes sense, but simply because God asks us to? A refined faith has charts and programs and plans. It's full of calculated steps and hand wringing. A refined faith is impressed with the big deals, big buildings, and big numbers. Certainly, God sometimes orchestrates big deals and provides for big buildings—but He is not counting heads. Instead, He counts the hairs on each head.

A reckless faith builds an ark before there's even a cloud in the sky. A reckless faith charges into the sea before thinking God may part the water. A reckless faith leaves ninety-nine sheep to go after one lost one. It does not need man's approval—or man's money. It honors God in the classroom, even when no one else there reveres Him. A reckless faith doesn't make moral compromises at the office, even when they're expected. A reckless faith believes in "til death do us part."

Reckless faith does not mean immature or unthinking. The truth is, the closer I grow to God, the more experiences and knowledge I accumulate, the more recklessly I desire to live. As a result, I want to ask God to heal my friend without mumbling that even if He doesn't, I'll try again later. I want to give away more than 10 percent since I know how to live comfortably with whatever is left over. I want to say *yes* to projects and relationships even when they sometimes don't make sense. I was commissioned that day on the border of Nicaragua and Costa Rica—but now I know my commission had nothing to do with clothes.

My commission is to have a childlike faith, so I can respond to holy nudges.

REFLECTION:

> *Do not despise these small beginnings, for the Lord*
> *rejoices to see the work begin . . .*
> – ZECHARIAH 4:10 (NLT)

What does this tell you about yourself? Others? God?

CHANGE:

What have you done, or are tempted to do, that would appear foolish to someone else? What does a holy nudge look like to you?

ACTION:

Do something unusual with your clothing today (wear your shirt inside out or backwards) as a reminder that sometimes God will ask us to look foolish for His sake.

21

The Grand V of Life
Yes to Staying Connected

EXPERIENCE:

Todd and I are like fireworks. Our relationship never coasts—it stalls and then bursts ahead. I didn't even know what I was looking for in a man, but I knew I had found it once we started dating.

One of the first guys I ever went out with was nice enough. One night he asked me where I'd like to eat, so I chose a new restaurant in town, and we had a great meal. We enjoyed that same restaurant for seven Saturdays—in a row. In his defense, he was just trying to please me. But from my perspective, I didn't find it engaging. If I'd married him, maybe I'd still be eating at that same restaurant.

Instead, I was longing for adventure—spiritual adventure—the kind where you understand you have one shot at life and you want to live it fully. That other man was godly in many ways, strong and stable, undoubtedly someone's ideal man. But not mine.

That same year, I met Todd. It was during this (immature) time that I invented an arbitrary measuring stick to decide whether I wanted to go out on a second date. I would judge my dates according to how decisively they ordered their food. If a date took too long deliberating over his order, I deemed him indecisive and preoccupied with unimportant details, and I wouldn't go out with him again.

When the waiter approached Todd on our first date, Todd ordered not only his meal, but mine as well—without even looking at the menu! How much more decisive can you get? Could this be the guide I needed for my lifelong journey? While some girls might have balked at someone taking control of what they were going to eat, I was drawn to his confidence, at the risk he took not knowing how I'd react. (To be clear: this was a one-time thing. From here on out, I would order for myself.)

Our personalities couldn't be more different, but God brought us together for a purpose. Simply put, we are better together than we are individually. Todd completes me and balances out every place where I fall short. When I sprint, he marathons. When he reacts, I respond. When I start, he finishes. When he thinks, I feel. When we decide to bring out the best in each other, it's breathtaking. But when we use our energy and emotions to bring the other down, it's ridiculous how fast the fire can burn the whole house down.

In an age when we are told to be healthy individuals, seeking self-fulfillment and avoiding dependency, the biblical model still holds true: the more we serve each other and become one flesh, the stronger—not weaker—we become. By marrying Todd, I've actually become more of who I was created to be, not less.

◦ ◦ ◦

One afternoon, I was coaching a small group as we did a team-building ropes course, and everyone (including me!) was frustrated. "Keep going, everyone. I am sure you are almost there!" I cheered half-heartedly. I was sure there was a point to our current challenge and believed our other staff member when he said it was *possible* to solve, but my patience had worn out along with my bug spray, and my cheering was waning in the afternoon sun.

The goal was to have two people, connected by their hands, balancing on two separate thin wires about a foot off the ground. The two wires form a V. The two people must stay on the wires from the bottom point of the V until the top, but as the space between them grows, so does the challenge. At the end of the V, the space between the two players is about nine feet wide. Pair after pair attempted the challenge, but everyone failed.

"How's it going?" My friend, our guide, approached us. I looked at him woefully. He leaned in to me and whispered, "Do you want to know the trick?"

I nodded. *Of course* I wanted to know the secret, if there was one!

"When you start at the point of the V, focus all your effort on keeping your partner up. Don't think about your own balance or self-preservation. As you focus on his balance, and he simultaneously on yours, you find equilibrium."

We spread the secret and sure enough, within minutes, every pair who had previously failed succeeded without much struggle. It made for interesting conversation on the way home: if we focused more on holding up our brothers and sisters and less on our own fears of falling (or who was looking at our fall), we would inevitably reach our goal— any goal—with less effort.

How many more people (family members? friends?) could we keep up on the wire across from us if we thought more about them and less about us? We live in a world where we so quickly "unfollow" people, create distance in relationships that require too much work, or draw boundaries when we feel uncomfortable. And when people we care about step off to self-preserve, we find a new partner and move on, disgusted with the failure, either theirs (which is judgement) or ours (which is shame). Could we stop our own journey long enough to grab our friend's, family member's, or partner's hand and help us both regain balance?

I have held the hands of friends, my mother, people older than me, younger than me, my color, not my color, my gender, not my gender, but of all those people, Todd is most often across from me in the Grand V of life. *Do I appreciate the risks he takes on my behalf? Do I allow him to talk to me honestly about struggles he sees in me? Do I ask him often enough to pray—with me, for me? Am I leaning in, straining for his success? Does his success matter to me as much as my own?*

Todd has been my personal guide to sanctification. Nothing has made me confront my own sin and selfishness as much as becoming one with someone else. For others, it's a child, a parent, a sibling, or a friend . . . whomever is across from you in life, and however they cause you to come face-to-face with your desire to self-preserve over self-sacrifice, we have a choice: We can either embrace self-denial and grow or resist it and find ourselves falling over and over again.

REFLECTION:

*Therefore encourage one another and build each other up,
just as in fact you are doing.*
– 1 THESSALONIANS 5:11

What does this truth tell you about yourself? Others? God?

CHANGE:

How much time do I spend in self-preservation? How do I practically help my brothers and sisters from falling?

ACTION:

Think about the person most often across from you on that V. Find one way to really support and encourage them today, and find one way you can ask them to help support you.

22

God Will Use Even This

Yes to Perspective

Hurricane Alex pummeled Monterrey, Mexico with almost forty inches of rain in as many hours. The city had widespread damage. Our little ministry campus felt under assault while the rain relentlessly demanded to go where it wanted.

I was outside, in the thick of the storm, bailing out buckets of rainwater alongside a motley crew of visiting guests, long-time staff friends, and some of the vulnerable teens that live with us. In the middle of it all, I stopped and realized what should have been crushing actually was joyful. We were fearful for our homes and mentally calculating the cost of damage as it was happening, but we were all in this together and were building a certain intimacy as we ganged up together against the storm. It was then—with dozens of us standing together, protecting the property and each other, wearing ponchos that had long since seemed useless, and sleep deprived to the point of being slap-happy—I realized: *God will use even this.* There is nothing, not even a hurricane, God can't work through to bring us good. I could choose to look at the rain and the mud, and focus on the worthless, or I could look at the deepening connection with friends and the fragile outreach to my neighbors and see some early fruit.

The turning point came around inch twenty. I had been wasting time wondering, *Why doesn't He stop it?* When, instead, I could have been marveling at God who allows all of creation the free will to live a life of our own choosing, and yet He still reaches down and redeems, repairs, restores.

The week after Hurricane Alex, we had to-do lists a mile long. As we began the cleanup process, I was determined to focus on the good that had, and would still, come from this storm. The celebration of provision, the delicate new connectedness we felt with neighbors around us, the intimacy in our ministry community, the reminder of what was really important, my list of the "good" was building.

I wrestled with that truth when tempted to look down at the septic water in my kitchen. I had a choice to learn how to pick up what felt heavy and watch it strengthen me, or let things in my life pin me down. It's more than looking on the bright side of things—which somehow implies when we grieve a loss or a sin, we are living on the dark side. Looking for God's work in the middle of hardship isn't about dark or light, it's not about mood or personality; it's about wisdom. It's not an attempt to brush over what is painful; it's an exercise in finding perspective, context, and hope.

There are scores of verses I read that implore us to "sit in the heavenly realms" (Ephesians 2:6), and "fix our eyes on Jesus" (Hebrews 12:2), and "set our minds on things above" (Colossians 3:2), and they are poetic and lyrical and mystical and beautiful. But are they applicable? What do those words even mean? How do we live in the midst of this broken world, getting our feet tripped up all sorts of places, and not look down more than we look up? When we find our story has taken on a dark chapter, either by our own wanderings or someone else's, do we close our eyes and muddle through? Do we just stay there, examining the consequential scars? Do we wait until our story has a bow on the end and can be properly considered a "testimony"?

There is a promise that God will work on our behalf, despite the circumstances and the other characters in our story—a promise the Enemy doesn't get the last word, and the scar we've incurred doesn't define us. It's a promise that whatever we might be experiencing today is just one chapter in a story He is writing and the story isn't over yet.

Jeremiah 15:19 says, "Therefore, thus says the LORD, 'If you return, then I will restore you—Before Me you will stand; And if you extract the precious from the worthless, You will become My spokesman'" (NASB). He is extracting the precious—precious promises, precious lessons, precious intimacy with Him—from the seemingly worthless circumstances, pain, situations, relationships, so we can be called His spokesmen. There are far more sticky situations in my day than miraculous moments. I want to hear and see and experience challenges and difficulties and setbacks and not immediately look down, but train my mind to set my thoughts on Him. That's key to our contentment.

As Christians, we should be marked by our radically different approach to life. We have access to a God who offers us peace, but some days the most conflicted people I talk to are believers. I am a vessel for an unending source of love; however, I can be guilty of wild judgment of those different from me. We have a God depositing into us all manner of wisdom; however, Christians can sound downright ignorant. I want my approach to challenges, to heartbreak, to failure to be a true reflection of my position in Christ.

The world says "follow your heart" and "speak your truth," but I say my heart can deceive me, and my mouth moves often without speaking Truth. I say, get my head in the right place, set my mind on His ways, and in that renewal, my heart will follow—no matter how strong the storm rages. Through the storm, He gives me His perspective to see the precious among the worthless.

REFLECTION:

Therefore, thus says the LORD, "If you return, then I will restore you—Before Me you will stand; And if you extract the precious from the worthless, You will become My spokesman. They for their part may turn to you, But as for you, you must not turn to them."
– JEREMIAH 15:19 (NASB)

What does this truth tell you about yourself? Others? God?

CHANGE:

Where have you had to extract the precious from the worthless? How do you fight for contentment?

ACTION:

Take a day off from social media or the radio, anything that creates "noise" in your life. Spend the time setting your mind on things above and remembering how God has grown you in hard circumstances.

23

We Had a Front Row Seat

Yes to the Unknown

EXPERIENCE:

I was in school in the US in 1986, when my twin girls, Marilin and Marlen, were being born in a village outside of Monterrey, Mexico. I wouldn't meet them until they were eleven years old and living in a children's home in Mexico. They'd come home permanently at age fifteen. While it's one of the best stories of my life, I can tell you from the start, it wasn't my idea.

One evening, when the twins were in junior high, Todd said to me, "Beth, what would you think if I said I have been wondering what it would be like to bring the twins here permanently?" He had just returned from a Father's Day event at their school, filling in as their father, and I thought maybe he'd had a few too many chili peppers.

"Like . . . as in, *all the time*? Adoption? Stay here with us?" I felt resistant, looking around at all the roles I was trying to balance and wondering if there was room for one more. He continued, "I think the Lord is asking us to make a commitment to the girls. I can feel it, and I want you to start praying about it."

I prayed, although a bit reluctantly at first. The *idea* of having them in our home, I thought, is more exciting than the *reality*. But whoever said "prayer is more for us than for God" was on to something. After a while, I felt my heart moving in the same direction. I tried to picture what it would look like to have them in our house, at our table, in our family pictures. I alternated between feeling excited and then terrified—and then both at the same time. There were lots of things I didn't know about raising teenagers, but having just been one a decade earlier, I thought *it couldn't have changed that much, could it?*

Sometimes, in those kinds of reckless-faith moments, the jump comes a split second before you're really sure there's water below. This was not one of those moments. This was a jump so high, I wouldn't know for years whether there was water below me. But then "it" comes over me, even while I'm panicking—that inexplicable, doesn't-make-sense-at-the-time, peace-that-passes-understanding feeling. Todd and

I stepped up to the edge, held hands, and jumped, offering the girls a permanent home with us within a month.

Now, they are college graduated, married with children, and delightful women whom I enjoy very much. But it was quite a road getting there. I erroneously assumed it would be hard, because it would be work teaching them to grow into what we thought was right. Wow! How many ways did God have to teach me that He always has more than one mission in mind? He used the girls to raise *me* up, just as much as He used us to raise them up. Taking in two teenage girls with their background and our lack of experience should have been a disaster, but God promises to be the Father to the fatherless. He has in every way co-parented with us. When we've needed wisdom, He has given it, and when we've needed patience or grace, He has always supplied it in abundance. And all of the sudden, my lack of enough and His more than sufficient became the good through line of this story. Who doesn't want more wisdom? Patience? Joy? Love? I do! And He used these girls to give it to me.

In those early days, when we struggled with communication and with the obstacles the girls' past put in our way, I reminded myself it was God's desire that we be a family, and He brought us together. I clung to Colossians 1:17, "He is before all things, and in him all things hold together."

I wish I could say that following God's will in building

our family led to many sweet days, and we sat around holding hands all the time. The truth is, our God cared so much about their healing, He was interested in doing whatever it took to bring their hurt spots to the surface. And we had a front-row seat.

In traditional parenting, you have years to teach your children to chew with their mouths shut or to write thank you notes; you have windows of time when they think you're the greatest, and you use those years to mold and influence their interests, spiritual worldviews, and even which sports team to cheer for. We quickly realized we could not cover fifteen years of parenting in our first year together. The girls would have felt like projects, and not people. I also didn't want their days to be filled with pointing out who they weren't, instead of who they were. So, we majored in the majors and let them eat how they wanted and dress how they felt most comfortable. We focused almost exclusively on their hearts.

Who were they sharing it with?

How did they respond to hurts?

When did they feel most alive?

Could they trust all that with Jesus?

In turn, we asked those same questions of ourselves, and once again God's will was multi-faceted. He not only wanted to wake their sleepy spirits, but, in the process, He wanted to woo ours as well. Did we have slammed doors and fights? Absolutely—about boys, dishes, curfews . . .

Did we cry at times? Yes—over misunderstandings, fear of the future, hurt feelings, unmet expectations. But God was building something we couldn't see, He saw their future generations, He saw the good work He'd prepared in advance for them to do. He saw girls He had created with a hope and a future. He saw a marriage made stronger through co-missioning.

He saw generations past, present, and future. He saw it all and was inviting us into something hard, but really good.

REFLECTION:

Seek the Kingdom of God above all else, and he will give you everything you need.
– LUKE 12:31 (NLT)

What does this truth tell you about yourself? Others? God?

CHANGE:

When is a time where you've stepped into the unknown and how did your faith grow from that experience? What has God used to bring your hurt spots to the surface?

ACTION:

Think of someone you believe needs to be reminded who

they are, and not who they aren't. Pray and ask the Lord to reveal something to you about them that is a gift, and then let them know.

24

Truth as Locust Repellent

Yes to Restoration

A year after the girls came to live with us, they were now sixteen and we all sat down on the living room floor, with a Bible in front of us, to do a check-up on our lives together. I turned to Joel 1:4 that illustrates God's promise to them and hoped the timing was right to share it: "What the gnawing locust has left, the swarming locust has eaten. And what the swarming locust has left, the creeping locust has eaten. And what the creeping locust has left, the stripping locust has eaten" (NASB). We asked if they could envision crops being eaten by locusts. We talked about how metaphorical locusts have buzzed into their lives, eating layer after layer—those were the locusts of abuse and neglect, of lies and other activities the Enemy uses to diminish God's glory.

I told them, "The book of Joel goes on to say in chapter two, verse thirteen, 'Now return to the Lord your God, for He is gracious and compassionate, slow to anger and abounding in lovingkindness and relenting of evil.' This is the key. I'm sure He will reveal to all of us the paths we need to take on our journey to healing, but the Bible is clear: the first step is to return to Him."

We spent the rest of the evening talking about their dreams and what returning to Him meant. We asked each of them, *What do you want to study? Where do you want to live? With whom? What kind of life can you imagine for yourself?*

We also talked about who in their lives have been locusts. What do locusts look like and how can we send them away when we hear them coming?

Todd prayed, "*Señor, be with our precious daughters whom you have created for a purpose. Help us to guide them down a path that offers more than we could ever ask or imagine. Amen.*"

I looked at Todd as he prayed, and I saw a completely different person than the Todd of just a year ago. He was more thoughtful, more sensitive, less willing to tolerate locusts. He was stronger, wiser, and fiercer to protect. A funny thing has happened as we have raised these girls: I like him more. In fact, being in over our heads has made us reach up to God, and, like the sides of a triangle, as we move upward, we can't help but draw closer together. We now laugh about memories no one else finds funny, or when one of the girls says something nobody but us gets. We feel protective when someone is insensitive towards them, and, most of all, we love hearing them call us "Mom" and "Dad."

A redeemed life, no less than the highest mountain, is a marker pointing to the Creator. Who but God can rebuild us into something stronger, using even the weakest part of our past to strengthen us?

In raising Marilin and Marlen, we had no idea where or how to begin. We would wake up in the middle of the night and ask for guidance: *What should we allow? What should we share? What things should we force them to do, and which should we let go?* Slowly, the buzzing of their locusts began to subside as the girls became better at hearing God whisper deep truths into their hearts, truths like:

You are valuable.
You are special.
You have a destiny.
You count.
You are gifted.
You were created for a purpose.
I have a plan for you.
You are my child.

These truths are like "locust repellent," and as the locusts disappear, we become more equipped to spot them whenever they approach again.

One day, years after we had read those passages from Joel together, I opened the Bible to that same chapter. God has a promise for all of us in the second chapter, which I didn't read to them at the time, because I wasn't sure they would have believed it. I have shown it to them since, and I know today the reality of this promise has taken root in the fertile soil of their hearts. Joel 2:25-26 says, "Then I will make up to you for the years that the swarming locust has eaten, the creeping locust, the stripping locust and the gnawing locust . . . You will have plenty to eat and be satisfied and praise the name of the Lord your God who has dealt wondrously with you . . ." (NASB).

He has made good on His promises—just as we knew He would. He is constantly making up for those years the locusts had eaten—in ways the girls will never forget. They have husbands now who love them, godly men who honor their history. They have daughters who will never fully understand the stories their mothers will tell them of their childhood. They have made peace with those years, and they have gained a strength they will carry forever.

As for me, it can take my breath away with how much God has moved in me through Marilin and Marlen. He taught me to jump when prompted and cry out when in over my head. He taught me I am capable of more than I thought and that love can make a family. Sometimes people unknowingly say, "Those girls are so lucky to have you." They, honestly, couldn't be more wrong. It's *we*—Todd and I—who are better, blessed, and grateful for the intertwining of our lives with the girls' lives.

REFLECTION:

Then I will make up to you for the years that the swarming locust has eaten, the creeping locust, the stripping locust and the gnawing locust . . . You will have plenty to eat and be satisfied and praise the name of the Lord your God who has dealt wondrously with you . . .
– JOEL 2:25–26 (NASB)

What does this truth tell you about yourself? Others? God?

CHANGE:

What locusts have come into your life? Where has God made good on His promises in your life?

ACTION:

Write one truth about who you are, according to the Bible, on an index card. Hang this locust repellent somewhere you can see daily.

25

We Can't Fix What God Wants to Heal

Yes to Pressing In

A friend of mine and I have a hashtag we've been using lately when we encounter Enemy activity: #damndevil. It's our way of signaling not everything is as we see it, and not every setback has a human to blame. There is opposition taking advantage of our sin, and to know it is to fight it. It doesn't surprise me anymore, but it doesn't get any easier. The devil is on the prowl, tearing up vulnerable children and marriages, preying on addictions, insecurities, and character flaws.

I once visited Key West, and went on a shark excursion. The way the crew drew the sharks to the boat was by pouring bloody fish into the water. The sharks were immediately drawn to the blood, and, as they feasted on the fish, I thought, *This is how the Enemy works. He is drawn to blood already in the water.* He doesn't say, "Oh, their bodies are breaking down, so I'll leave their marriage alone," or "Their children are struggling, I will leave their friendships intact." No, he sees tension and fatigue, and he gets a foothold. The foothold, left unattended, becomes a stronghold, until we fight the sin that makes us prey with the Truth of God's Word.

The Enemy is a double-downer and he leaves a wake of hard stories wherever he attacks—people in chaos, in need of God's peace and intervention. However, as strong and dark as the Enemy can appear, Exodus 8:19 teaches there is more power in even the "finger of God."

I had a friend going through a hard time recently, the kind without an end in sight and no easy answers. I didn't know what to do or say, so it was tempting to walk away or avoid her. But as a Christian, I shouldn't want to disconnect from her, I should be able to have close proximity to pain. I can get close to it, because the Bible tells me what to do with it. God instructs Moses how to build a tabernacle and tells him that if they make room for Him, He will come and fill the space (Exodus 25). That's what He is saying to us today. If we'll make room for Him, He'll come with whatever is needed into the bloody waters of our lives. If my friend needs protection, strength, peace . . . it's not up to me to give it to her. It's up to me to come near and hold her hands, and we've now created twice the space for God to fill.

I've admittedly had a steep growth curve while becoming fluent in hard stories. I can wrestle with wanting to see something or someone broken become unbroken, and so I dedicate energy towards putting it back together. But God is teaching me that we can't fix what He wants to heal. When He heals, the result is stronger and the impact greater. When I try and fix something or, worse yet, someone, I usually just cover up or distract from what God wants to do in them (or me).

While I am busy with worry, *Will this ever get better? What will happen next? Can they handle it?* God is sitting on His throne, privy to the whole story and perfect in His timing. The mark of fluency in hard stories is the confidence God has not forgotten the people we are called to love. He doesn't wring His hands and doesn't want us to tap out. His work is a long play. Our culture begs for instant gratification, and I can be guilty of thinking, *Why isn't this getting easier or the situation improving?* However, faith and ministry are much like a muscle. The more I exercise, the stronger I am. I can be tempted to give up, but people are always worth it, and if God's asking me to engage, He'll strengthen me for the task. And, in the way only He can, He'll use it to increase my growth as well.

I get most tired or discouraged when I think it's up to me to save someone or something. I've made this rookie mistake more times than I want to recount. I was certain if

I didn't do something, all would be lost. I now know better: there is only one shelter to rest under, and there is only one Savior who died on a cross. Anything I offer, I do so as His ambassador. He does the prompting, calling, empowering, rescuing, and saving.

Jesus forgives, Jesus directs, Jesus comforts. He provides answers, He convicts. This is His job. I can step into a role that isn't mine far too easily, especially when someone willingly puts me there. I won't do this again; the consequences are grave. Hard stories should draw us to Jesus, not to man. We are at our best when we continually reinforce this truth. I can want to give someone something or meet a need only God can, but it ends up only making the story messier. Whether I am frustrated with a chapter of a story I'm invested in or unhappy with the timing of something, I have no choice but to rest in the truth that He is sovereign. It's the most reckless form of faith we can have: Trust Him and His timing. If He allowed it, He has a purpose for it. If something or someone isn't moving on our timetable, we can trust God, who has a better perspective; He is working on what we cannot see. The peace I crave sits on top of this truth: He is in control and can be trusted.

In the end, what makes the shark, or whatever metaphor you want to call the Enemy, go away is pressing in to Jesus, pressing in to the Truth. We all need more truth and less pretense in our lives. We live in a world where we hear what we want to and we tune out what we don't like. In a hard story, we have the privilege of reminding ourselves and everyone involved: Jesus is the lifeline in bloody waters. The Bible is the plumb line and all decisions should sit level on it. If something doesn't align with Scripture, it's spiritual dissonance. We can say *yes* to pressing in to hard stories, knowing He's given us all we need.

REFLECTION:

Do not fear, for I have redeemed you; I have summoned you by name; you are mine. When you pass through the waters, I will be with you; and when you pass through the rivers, they will not sweep over you . . .
– ISAIAH 43:1-2

What does this truth tell you about yourself? Others? God?

CHANGE:

Where do you have to trust Him today for His timing? How can you press into the hard stories of the people around you?

ACTION:

Grab a friend and say a prayer together for each other or a common friend. Ask Jesus to fill the space you've created with His gifts.

26

Obedience over Comfort
Yes to Strength

EXPERIENCE:

I know a woman who just by living her life has mentored me. She runs a children's home in Mexico, and has for many years. She's one of those people who has walked with God so long and so well that I just like to be near her. I want some of the peace and strength she's found in Jesus to jump over onto me. People are drawn to Martha, not for what's on the surface, but for what lies underneath. God has built within her layer upon layer of faith. I wanted to peel back some of those layers, so I asked her how it all started. How did she gain her ability to choose character over what feels comfortable? How did she learn such reckless faith?

She begins, "I found myself alone late in life, and I became drawn to people who needed mercy. I simply wanted to focus on others and I started in the jails and the slums. I used to stand up in church and tell everyone that on the weekend I was going to this jail or that drug house, and I'd practically beg people to come with me. But they wouldn't. So, for four or five years, I went mostly alone to minister."

"Were you ever in danger? Were you afraid?" I lean forward, curious.

"I was more afraid of what would happen to me if I stayed home than if I went!" she laughs. "As God would have it, He left me feeling dissatisfied; He gave me a sense there was something else to come. Eventually, He directed me to minister to orphans."

"Did you have people telling you that you should just live out the rest of your retirement in peace? That you deserved it? Earned it?" I ask.

"Oh, yes, most people tried to stop me, though I don't know why. I feel most alive when I am ministering. I think some people just found it too tiring to worry about me," she said. She faced many challenges at the beginning—land, staff, and these were burdens she lifted daily to the Lord. "*If this is what you want . . .*" her prayers would always begin. Slowly, the pieces started falling into place. Land was donated, staff appeared, funding trickled in—just enough to open her doors. She found herself dipping into her own savings many months to balance the books. "But it's all the

Lord's money anyway," she insists.

Wouldn't it be great if after we make a difficult choice, after we start down a path of God's leading, our affirmation would come in the form of easy days and easy ways? As I listen to Martha talk about her orphanage's beginnings, I wonder whether struggle is the confirmation we're on the right road, and whether blue skies are actually a warning. I suggest this to Martha. She replies, "We are in work opposed by the Enemy." Then she smiles as she adds, "It's all worth it, though, when I walk out of the office and hear shouts of 'Mamá Martha.'" She has been *mamá* to hundreds of children in the twenty years since her home opened its doors. Patiently and quietly, she has lifted their eyes from their circumstances, up to a God who she believes has a purpose for every life.

She tells another story: "A couple of years ago, I woke up at 3:00 a.m. feeling a burden for some unpaid bills. I told the Lord, 'I am the servant; You are the King. If You provide for Your work, I will gladly continue, but I cannot muster it up anymore.'

"The next morning, your husband, Todd, came to tell me of a sponsor who agreed to cover the orphanage's expenses for at least a year. Ever since that day, I wake up every morning at 3:00 a.m. to read my Bible and remember what the Lord did that night."

That's Martha—character over comfort.

Now in her eighties, she still works at the children's

home, but admits to occasional fatigue. "There'll be time to rest on the other side," she tells me when I voice concern, "But today, there's still work to do."

As I drive home that day after listening to Martha's story, I think about the truth I learned from her. She doesn't view herself as God's teammate as she reaches out to the children in her home. She sees herself as an extension of God's care. They aren't working in tandem; God is the Source, and she is the outlet. And what He has to offer will never run out.

Life had offered her two choices. One looked more appealing—with less work, less pain, less stress, and less heartache. It would have been the socially acceptable thing to do, and a relief to those around her, if she had just quietly lived out her retirement in peace. But she chose a harder path, and although it's been tough, by her own testimony, she feels richer, fuller, more satisfied, more loved, more alive. Who wouldn't want that quality of life?

We are constantly advised to take care of ourselves (which is important) and to maintain balance (which has value), but it can be tempting to stop when the Spirit is still saying "Go!" Instead of listening to ourselves and knowing our own limitations, shouldn't we listen to the Spirit and heed His direction? Sometimes that might look like stillness when we want activity. Sometimes that means avoiding activities that produce stress and self-importance. Still, sometimes that means working when you're tired, listening when you have other plans, or giving up when you'd rather not. It means understanding that on your own, you cannot help or listen or serve or share or work or accomplish anything of value if it's not done with God's strength.

REFLECTION:

And without faith it is impossible to please God, because anyone who comes to him must believe that he exists and that he rewards those who earnestly seek him.
– HEBREWS 11:6

What does this truth tell you about yourself? Others? The Lord?

CHANGE:

Where have you had to choose between obedience and comfort? How do you remember what God's done for you?

ACTION:

Think about something God has provided for you. What can you do to regularly remember to thank Him? Could you set an alarm? Leave a post-it note on your mirror? Create a trigger so you'll be in the pattern of gratitude for your blessings.

27

Hope We Make It

Yes to Letting Go

EXPERIENCE:

It was basketball try-out season in my son's junior high and it was giving me plenty of teachable moments. I just assumed when this process started, those teachable moments would be more directed at my son and less towards me. We were new to the school district, after having lived out of the country for his entire life, in a place where basketball wasn't an organized sport.

So here we were, a thirteen-year-old boy, bursting with hope, in a gym full of fifty candidates fighting for a spot on a bench that would only hold twelve. I started early with the *are-you-sure-this-is-what-you-want* questions. The answer was an emphatic *yes*. Then I followed up with my husband, "Can you teach him everything he needs to know this week?" The answer was an emphatic *no*. I sat and waited, watching for signs of rejection or discouragement, wanting to protect and prevent any negative emotion from coming his way. What is it about parenting that makes me want to cushion the hard and difficult? Is this how Jesus is with me? Does He see the places I put myself out there and want me to not feel pain? Or does He know good growth sometimes comes from hard lessons?

The weeks of open gym start. One day, I am early to pick him up, ready for his tears with the milkshake I collected on the way to school. Instead, his response was positive, and I found myself sucking down the chocolaty goodness, needing it more than him. *Do I think his performance or approval reflects me in some way?*

The day came when they made the cuts. I started the day with prayer and felt the peace God had been offering me for weeks, but I had rejected. I wanted to control or, worse yet, manipulate the situation to avoid my son feeling discomfort. This is not reality; my son's realistic understanding of his abilities and this opportunity are an exercise of risk taking I ultimately want him to do more of. I believe exercising this muscle will benefit him in the years to come. Offering himself and feeling okay with the results is a sign of maturity, so why would I wish away this chance for him to grow? Because if he has to risk, that means I do too. If he has to face rejection, so do I. If he isn't good enough, maybe I am not either. The reality of that confession is ugly. Those fears could win this war, but I won't let them. Reckless faith has to be okay with risk, because whether there's victory or not, there's always growth. And growth is good. I have to believe and trust regardless of whose names are posted on the gym door, life is about leaning in, doing your best, and believing the results are a part of a sovereign plan.

Settled in my heart, I dropped him off that morning with these words, "I am so glad we're trying out for basketball, Josh."

"*We* are trying out, Mom?" he teased me, smiling, "hope *we* make it." He was on to me, and frankly that wasn't a good sign. A teenage boy needs to be working towards independence, and my broken emotions peeking through, enough so that he perceived them, weren't helping.

The world's messaging and my temperament, combined with upbringing and influence, all swirl together to make me feel responsible for *so much*. Basketball try-outs in the scheme of things, aren't a big deal, but it highlighted my irrational need to want everything and everyone to be happy, all the time. Since that's an impossibility, then I would either need to let go or go crazy trying to make it happen.

Are you tired? Worn out? Burned out on religion? Come to me. Get away with me and you'll recover your life. I'll show you how to take

a real rest. Walk with me and work with me—watch how I do it.
Learn the unforced rhythms of grace. I won't lay anything heavy
or ill-fitting on you. Keep company with me and you'll learn to live
freely and lightly.
– MATTHEW 11:28-30 (MSG)

Could it be that He had a plan for me to work alongside of Him, and not carry what wasn't mine? That the rhythm of my day could be graceful, and what *was* put on me not ill-fitting? I wanted most of all to have a life lived freely and lightly, so this means trusting in One who sees it all and directs our paths.

Josh didn't make the basketball team. But not making the basketball team led to him trying indoor track where he hurdled for the first time. Track became his passion, and will lead him next year to a college team where he'll hurdle his heart out, risking, pursuing, and trusting Jesus who loves him.

REFLECTION:

Keep company with me and you'll learn to live freely and lightly.
– MATTHEW 11:30 (MSG)

What does this truth tell you about yourself? Others? God?

CHANGE:

What have you put on that was ill-fitting? Where have you felt responsible for someone else?

ACTION:

Put on a piece of clothing that is ill-fitting. Look in a mirror or take a picture of yourself. Donate it as a symbol of shedding what doesn't belong on you.

28

The Jar is Not Empty
Yes to Looking Upward

EXPERIENCE:

I grew up near an amusement park, and, as soon as I turned sixteen, I applied to work on the biggest, fastest, longest wooden roller coaster in the world. I knew everything there was to know about "The Beast" and rode it a dozen times a day for a couple of summers. Even though I could anticipate every turn, what always got me was the feeling in my stomach right before I went down the first hill. Riding seventy miles per hour on a wooden roller coaster twelve times a day sounds like foolishness now, but I don't want to ever outgrow the yearning to feel alive.

I was on a path I thought was exciting, I was seeing

needs and helping meet them and feeling good in the middle, but God has more than that in mind for us. He is not only the star of every story, but the principle orchestrator, and He wants my faithfulness above all else. Now I'm on a path where God does what He does, and simply uses me to accomplish His plan when and where He sees fit—and more needs are being met than I could have ever have met by myself.

Like that roller coaster, it still takes my breath away.

It wasn't the *country* of Mexico that changed me, it was being somewhere I couldn't control, didn't understand, felt overwhelmed by, was powerless in, and broken for the needs of the people there. For the first time, *I* wasn't enough and what I saw, I couldn't fix. I couldn't look inward, for I knew I didn't have answers. I couldn't look outward, it was hard and confusing. I only could look upward, and there God showed me He's been intervening in desperate stories for a long time.

Then the word of the Lord came to him: "Go at once to Zarephath in the region of Sidon and stay there. I have directed a widow there to supply you with food." So he went to Zarephath. When he came to the town gate, a widow was there gathering sticks. He called to her and asked, "Would you bring me a little water in a jar so I may have a drink?" As she was going to get it, he called, "And bring me, please, a piece of bread." "As surely as the Lord your God lives," she replied, "I don't have any bread—only a handful of flour in a jar and a little olive oil in a jug. I am gathering a few sticks to take home and make a meal for myself and my son, that we may eat it—and die." Elijah said to her, "Don't be afraid. Go home and do as you have said. But first make a small loaf of bread for me from what you have and bring it to me, and then make something for yourself and your son. For this is what the Lord, the God of Israel, says: "The jar of flour will not be used up and the jug of oil will not run dry until the day the Lord sends rain on the land."

– 1 KINGS 17:8-14

The widow did as Elijah had told her and there was food every day for Elijah, the woman, and her family. She wasn't in control anymore; in her moment of desperation she looked upward. The jar of flour was not used up, and the jug of oil did not run dry, in keeping with the Word of the Lord.

God is inviting us to trust Him, trust that He will care for us. Imagine how the widow's heart swelled knowing God looked down into her home and saw her situation. He asked her to have a reckless faith and trust in a man she had never met, to give away all she had left. When she walked out on that limb, God did more than catch her from falling; He lifted her up and provided for her.

I had started my missionary life just asking God to show up. It was a bare minimum request. Over the course of many years and a ridiculous amount of hard lessons, I see now it's effortless for Him to show off. He delights in supernatural demonstrations, it's all He is and all He can do, because He is otherworldly. The limitations of this earth aren't His limitations, He can do whatever He wants, whenever and wherever and however He wants. Read on to see what He did for this woman's son:

Some time later the son of the woman who owned the house became ill. He grew worse and worse, and finally stopped breathing. She said to Elijah, "What do you have against me, man of God? Did you come to remind me of my sin and kill my son?" "Give me your son," Elijah replied. He took him from her arms, carried him to the upper room where he was staying, and laid him on his bed. Then he cried out to the Lord, "Lord my God, have you brought tragedy even on this widow I am staying with, by causing her son to die?" Then he stretched himself out on the boy three times and cried to the Lord, "Lord my God, let this boy's life return to him!" The Lord heard Elijah's cry, and the boy's life returned to him, and he lived. Elijah picked up the child and carried him down from the room into the house. He gave him to his mother and said, "Look, your son is alive!" Then the woman said to Elijah, "Now I know that you are a man of God and that the word of the Lord from your mouth is the truth."
– 1 KINGS 17:17-24

Did the widow doubt God's provision and protection after that? Maybe on some days when she, like all of us, let her thoughts get the best of her. But I have a hunch she told more than a few people about how her son's life was saved; maybe she even invited them in for some bread. That's what happens when God meets your need; you can't shut up about it. Reckless faith is stunning. It is the stuff stories are told about years later. God is calling us to give to others recklessly because that *is His nature*. He could have atoned for our sins many other ways, or just kept accepting our livestock on the altar, but He demonstrated the ultimate example in reckless giving when He offered His body for us.

He is doing more than fetching what we ask; He is orchestrating events that are multipurposed. He is blessing the receiver, the provider, the asker, the observer, the second-hand hearer; He is big and alive and dynamic and involved. When I remember this, I can skim along the top of life and trust He has what I need, and it's mine for the asking. When I forget, I expend a ridiculous amount of energy gathering for myself what I think will make me feel better.

What is He asking me for, and how will I exchange that which I hold back for that which He offers without end? By looking up and being expectant.

REFLECTION:

Then the woman said to Elijah, "Now I know that you are a man of God and that the word of the Lord from your mouth is the truth."
 – 1 KINGS 17:24

What does this truth tell you about yourself? Others? The Lord?

CHANGE:

How have you seen God care for you? When do you doubt His provision?

ACTION:

Cook with some oil today, and, as you pour it out, remember this biblical truth: God will multiply His resources on your behalf.

29

Divine Appointments
Yes to Being Interrupted

God always has more than one mission going on at a time.

Semana Santa, the week before Easter, is the busiest week of the year in Mexico. Since the crucified Christ is the preeminent symbol of faith to this Catholic nation, the celebrations of that week are even more important than Christmas. The whole country goes on spring break, adults and children alike, and there is a party on every street corner.

Todd and I have agreed to host eighty people from Oklahoma at our mission that week. Since we can't ignore what is happening in the city, and just going about our normal business would make no sense, we engaged our visitors with the culture and did an outreach in a busy suburb of the city. We also want the children of the orphanage to participate in an outreach experience, so we round up our eighty visitors from Life Church in Oklahoma, along with several dozen children from the children's home. Arriving in the suburb, we stream out of the buses on a hot Saturday afternoon, carrying two thousand cold Cokes and invitations to a passion play our Mexican church is presenting at a local theater later that evening. That is our plan, and I am convinced it is also God's design for the day. I plan not to stray from it.

As we break into teams, I sit in a central location and, with my clipboard and my visor and my unchangeable goal, I supervise. But about halfway through the afternoon, I'm called over to solve a problem. On my way, I bump into a woman and mutter, "*Con permiso*," and not to be deterred, I keep on going. I'm there to pass out invitations. This is the big deal—an impressive plan. Meanwhile, one of the young men from Oklahoma, who is trailing along in the wake of my determination, tries to strike up a conversation with the woman I brushed by. After exhausting his Spanish, he comes to get my attention. "That lady over there . . . I think she said she either *has* an orphanage or *is one* or *has visited one* or *wants one* . . . I don't know . . . something along those lines. I think you should talk to her." I look at him and then close my eyes in response to the hair now standing up on my neck—which is a big deal considering the amount of sweat there. Before I even turn around, I can feel the Holy Spirit stir me. I sigh, adjust my visor, glance at my clipboard, and hand it off to someone else. When I turn around, more than two dozen little children, all dressed alike, are standing behind this woman, staring at me.

That afternoon I meet Mama Cony and the children who live with her. For more than two decades, she and her husband, Chuy, have provided shelter to children who have nowhere else to go. On the day I meet her, almost forty of them live in Mama Cony and Chuy's little house. God in heaven knows she and her husband have some tremendous responsibilities and needs, and they have cried out to God and trusted Him to bring help.

On that day, once Mama Cony had put matters into God's hands and stopped wringing her own, she took her children on a walk on a beautiful afternoon during *Semana Santa*. That day marked the beginning of our partnership with Mama Cony.

Today, Mama Cony's ministry serves more than four times as many children as she did on the day we met. She now has three children's homes instead of one, and probably has plans for three more. God was writing a story in heaven for the children living with Mama Cony, and His grand plan to protect them involved a chance meeting on a hot afternoon in Mexico during *Semana Santa*.

The young man from Oklahoma set off a chain of

events that led to us fulfilling a God-ordained destiny. Boy, am I ever glad he chose to try out his Spanish! We had a divine appointment that afternoon—but I had almost missed the plan because I was so busy with my own plan and agenda. It's not that the two thousand Cokes weren't used by God. I am sure they were. Someday in heaven, I will find out which of those recipients of a Coke and an invitation to the play came forward to profess faith in Christ. He isn't limited by only one plan. God was also prompting a teenager from Oklahoma to be bolder about his faith. And God had a lesson or two for me as well. And one for Mama Cony to boot.

Isn't it hard to let go of our plans? Sometimes I'm so sure of myself, so confident that whatever is hardest to pull off, whatever is splashier or pays the biggest returns, must be God's plan. Sometimes I think God looks at the little boy with the loaves, instead of the grown man with the fancy plans (John 6). He looks at the woman with the perfume bottle, rather than the spiritual leader hosting the lunch (Mark 14). He looks at the boy with the sling, rather than the army (1 Samuel 17).

Is He trying to get my attention while I am distracted by Coke bottles and my own plans? I want my eyes to be open to all He is doing around me.

REFLECTION:

For the LORD will go before you, And the God of
Israel will be your rear guard.
– ISAIAH 52:12

What does this truth tell you about yourself? Others? God?

CHANGE:

When is it hardest for you to be interrupted? Where do you see God doing more than one thing at a time?

ACTION:

Write down all your plans for tomorrow. Have you left room for Him to rearrange your agenda? Set an alarm for some time in the day tomorrow when you can stop and pray for God to reveal His more-than-one-mission-at-a-time plan for you.

30

The Best We Can Be Is Still to Come

Yes to Dreaming

EXPERIENCE:

"Go on, fight him," taunts one of the boys. *But I don't want to fight anyone,* Isaac thinks, hoping the attention will just go away.

"You afraid? Where did you come from anyway, that you don't know how to fight?"

More of them gather to look at the new kid in the orphanage. As he balls his hands into fists, Isaac thinks, *Afraid? Yes. But not of you. I'm afraid I'll hurt you.* BAM! He knocks down the boy who's chanting the loudest. *Better to hurt them before they hurt you.* He thinks about his three little brothers. That morning his mother told him, "Isaac, go see if it's a good place for me to bring your younger brothers." It is the second children's home Isaac has been sent to in a year. "You know I need you to check it out first," says his mom. *I will do this for my brothers*, Isaac thinks as he falls asleep. *I'll make everyone here afraid of me so when my brothers come, they won't be bothered.*

One night, while walking by the cafeteria, I see Isaac quietly drawing. He doesn't know I'm there, and he looks so peaceful. He's leaning against the wall, lost in his notebook. Something about what he's doing makes his face look different. I should feel guilty about spying on him, but I can't look away. A noise alerts him, and he shoves his drawing into his backpack. *No one saw you, Isaac*, I thought, *your tough guy reputation remains intact.*

. . .

It's time for Isaac's junior high graduation, and he needs to decide about his future. He seems to have two choices, and they are equally uninspiring.

"I could leave and get a job," he told us, "or I can go to a technical school. Everyone tells me I should go to work in a factory and earn money. Then I could help out my family . . . but I'm not sure what to do—or what I want to do."

"Isaac, you know you could continue your studies," Todd says. "We'd love to have you around here longer."

"Maybe I'll enroll at the vocational high school," Isaac

says, looking away. "I found a school I could do okay in."

My heart both leaps and sinks. I know he's a gifted and creative artist and I had hoped he'd consider architecture or graphic arts, but his sub-par junior high grades loom in the background. He's a big boy, with a strong stature, and going into "the arts" wasn't on his radar. While some of the other boys in his class were among our first students to consider a college-preparatory high school program, Isaac shuffled off to classes that satisfied other people's expectations for his life. For a boy with his background, learning a practical skill seemed like the "right thing."

Finally, as his graduation from the tech high school approaches, I say, "Isaac, we're proud of you. What do you want to do now?"

"What do I want to do? Draw! That's all I've ever wanted to do. I love commercials and cartoons. I like ads and design." His voice sounds animated. "Where can I go and study *that*?"

I want to hug him for being honest, and slug him for waiting until the week of graduation to admit it.

"Sure, there's a place to study drawing," I respond, "but first you have to go to college-prep high school—the track you didn't choose two years ago. That means going into a classroom with fifteen-year-olds, and you'll be eighteen, then adding a college degree on top of it." I look at him pleadingly, "Do you want it? Enough that when it's hard, you just do it anyway? It'll take tremendous energy to change your study habits, your expectations of yourself, your capacity to meet new people and be in new environments. You'll have to change your work ethic, how you spend your time and with whom you spend your time, how you spend your money . . ." I needed him to understand. "Do you want the big change—the future, a job you love—enough to start with all these daily little changes?"

His big brown eyes looked so vulnerable. He drops his fist into his other hand and says, "Yes!"

Isaac changed tremendously after that day, although I wonder if change isn't becoming more of who you've never been, and instead building upon who you have always been. Maybe change is reversing the world's impact on and destruction of who God made you to be. Eventually, reckless faith grew into desiring the upheaval of change, believing the best he could be is still to come. Every time Isaac faced a challenge (a deadline, a hard professor, a snotty group partner, less money than he wanted for materials), he had a choice: either keep at it or quit. Choosing to stay built confidence where before there was only fear. It's the kind of confidence that doesn't have to strike the other guy first.

Isaac's most reckless faith moment came the day he enrolled at the prestigious CEDIM University, world-renowned for its graphic design program. It was his way of saying to the world that he had a gift and was willing to share it—a far cry from the boy hiding behind the building with his notebook. The old Isaac would have settled for any program where he could finish under the radar. But the maturing, changing, engaging Isaac was ready for another risk. His reckless faith saw him through as a graduate four years later.

All throughout biblical history, God's called the least likely into new places. He asked a reluctant Moses to go back to Egypt to take on a role he didn't believe he deserved. When God used Moses to bring plagues against Egypt, or raise his right hand at the edge of the Red Sea, or ask for manna in the desert, or deliver the Ten Commandments, Moses knew acutely that he didn't have what it took for what God was asking.

Striving towards what you believe is ahead requires faith. Faith gives birth to dreams we might be the only ones who can see, dreams that God planted in us to fulfill. The best stories come from steps we take just outside of what's comfortable or expected. Isaac taught me that.

REFLECTION:

> *For I am the LORD your God who takes hold of your right hand and says to you, Do not fear; I will help you.*
> – ISAIAH 41:13

What does this truth tell you about yourself? Others? God?

CHANGE:

How do we reverse the world's impact on who God has made us to be? How do you face change? What fears stand in the way of what God is calling you to do?

ACTION:

Write your fear on a rock and throw it into a creek, lake, or ocean signifying that God is bigger than the fears you have.

31

Rays of Light
Yes to Wholeness

I am eating breakfast when one member of the Mexican staff comes in to tell me about her Sunday lunch. "I went with my family to the chicken stand, and we were all sitting there eating our chicken, when I felt the Holy Spirit prompt me to talk to a woman who was there with her large family. I wish I could say I went right over, but I didn't. All the way home I was chiding myself for not following through. Once I got home, the Spirit would not let me rest, so I explain to my husband we have to go back in case she's still there. And you know what? She was still there. I walked up and just told her the Lord has directed me to her, and I asked if there is anything she would like me to pray for. She laughed and told me that she and her husband have a small orphanage and she would appreciate people coming to visit."

"Can you believe that?" she finishes. "We need to go and visit their home. We just have to." She looks at me in a way that feels urgent.

We make a date to go to see their home, and my first impression is that it's incredibly small. I notice the walls don't reach the roof, there aren't enough beds, the refrigerator's empty, and a myriad of other problems that signal the extreme poverty of those who live here. *Lord, where do we start?* Just then a little girl walks up beside me and puts her arms up for a hug. I smile, knowing I was just sent the answer.

Puri, the woman whom my friend saw at the chicken stand, and her husband, Esteban, run this home. They have taken in a couple dozen children and live daily by God's manna. As the afternoon progresses, I have the privilege to hear more of their story, how God led them after a long season of infertility to their first baby girl, and then the next five, and now dozens; how in this home, called *Rayos de Luz* ("Rays of Light") the children feel grateful to be in a place where they are loved, safe, and fed every day. Their situation demands a new level of understanding from me. The work they do and the conditions under which they serve would break most of us in a week or so, and yet they have cheerfully committed to a lifetime of service.

I am impressed by the heroes of the faith, people who

sign up *for their whole life* for service. Amy Carmichael served orphans in India for decades without a furlough. Corrie ten Boom ran her ministry until she died at an old age. Mother Theresa had an impact all over the world. The list is long and many names are not well-known. Are these people superhuman servants who deserve to be up on a pedestal? Or did they simply learn along the way how to tap into what Puri and Esteban have discovered?

I took my niece to *Rayos de Luz* last week. Puri met us at the door with a little girl who had just arrived the day before. She wasn't quite two years old, and her eyes were full of fear. "Isn't she beautiful?" coos Puri. I agree and shake my head as I embrace Puri, wondering how she divides herself in so many pieces. Then I remember something I heard in church once as a child. God is not part loving, part graceful, part peaceful, part forgiving. Instead, He is *all loving* on top of *all graceful* on top of *all peaceful*. He is not divided up so we each get a piece; we all get all of Him, all the time.

My mind wanders to my home, where Todd and I are currently parenting many children. How can I be more like God, instead of trying to break myself up in equal size pieces for everyone, which never feels good or works out right anyway? What if, instead, I could be all myself, wholly offered to Him, so He can spill out enough onto my family? *Is that how Puri does it?* I wonder as I walk away. *Does she just look at God, and ask Him to look at all twenty of them?*

When my car needs work, the traffic is bad, or it won't

stop raining . . . when I am tempted to sit down and complain about anything that's inconvenient or seemingly impossible, I remember the little "rays of light" who live in abundance in places like *Rayos de Luz*. More than any paycheck or possession, what God offers me makes me rich, and His strength is more than enough for any work He has prepared in advance for me. This is the spiritual rhythm that keeps me going, I can walk into a meeting, or a conversation, or even a conflict and think to myself, *I don't know how this is going to work out* . . . Then I can decide to look up to God and feel Him empower me. So, I say to Him:

> *I believe in You.*
> *I need You.*
> *Come for me.*

And then I wait.

I can let go of trying to make it all work, of creating my own kingdom, of proving myself or killing myself trying. I can let go of escape routes and back-up plans, excuses and false promises, measuring and dividing my energy and my time. I can let go and let God be all He promised to be.

REFLECTION:

> *He is before all things, and in him all things hold together.*
> – COLOSSIANS 1:17

What does this truth tell you about yourself? Others? God?

CHANGE:

Where do you feel pulled in many directions? What do you need more of that God can provide?

ACTION:

Choose something you will set aside to give someone today. Maybe it's five dollars or twenty minutes of undistracted time. Ask God to show you when, where, and to whom to give that gift.

32

A Page from Our Script

Yes to Discipline

EXPERIENCE:

"If you can't share it, you can't have it." This is one of our family scripts and I only have to start the first two words before my kids chime in together to finish it. We have other family quotes, "Do it right, or do it over" and "Speak words of life, not death." These sayings and the stories that accompany them are all a part of our family culture. They reinforce over and over again certain values and cement our family identity.

Family scripts are invaluable in creating community amongst a group of people. What do we stand for? And how does it compare with the messages of our larger society? How does our calendar and spending, our words and actions, reflect these values? Throughout biblical history, there have been creeds, truths memorized by a group of faithful believers to reinforce and remind them of what they believe to be true. This is what we hold onto when circumstances challenge us to compromise.

Todd and I are intentional about these life scripts, although he's admittedly much better at it than I am. Here's a few from our list:

Lazy people don't eat. I feel like our children knew this biblical principle before they learned to sing the alphabet. It was important to Todd for our children to learn how to participate in meal prep and clean up, and see themselves as contributors in our household, not consumers. 2 Thessalonians 3:10 says, "For even when we were with you, we gave you this rule: 'The one who is unwilling to work shall not eat.'"

Don't kick someone while they are down. This came up at dinner tables and in staff meetings. It was conversation when watching the news or sports. This is so ingrained in Todd that, as he grew in leadership over the years, I've watched him *lean into* hard stories, instead of more safely distancing himself. I pray our children, and the children we love around the world, grow up looking for how they can bring *shalom* to someone's chaos. Isaiah 35:3 says, "Encourage the exhausted, and strengthen the feeble" (NASB).

Do it right, or do it over. This has been written on countless worksite clipboards and made into a half-dozen T-shirt designs. My children know it applies to chores, homework, thank you notes, and apologies. Colossians 3:23-24 says, "Whatever you do, work heartily, as for the Lord and not for men, knowing that from the Lord you will receive the inheritance as your reward. You are serving the Lord Christ" (ESV).

Be humble, be a learner. There is so much Todd and I have learned since 1997, when our Back2Back and parenting journey simultaneously began. We've learned another language, how to raise funds, how to parent children from hard places, how to listen to God's voice, and how to be leaders, learners, and teachers. I endeavor for our children to see this I-don't-know-it-all attitude as an example. Colossians 3:12 says, "Therefore, as God's chosen people, holy and dearly loved, clothe yourselves with compassion, kindness, humility, gentleness and patience."

Be vocal about how you need God. I am working always on spiritual transparency. I don't want our kids to think being a Christian means we are supposed to pretend to have it all together, but instead I hope they hear us regularly ask God for wisdom, discernment, self-control, mercy, patience, and peace. John 15:5 says, "I am the vine; you are the branches. If you remain in me and I in you, you will bear much fruit; apart from me you can do nothing."

Show up for each other. Our children have watched Todd jump on airplanes for staff needs, work long hours, and still attend their school events. We want to be intentional about presence when absence is more expected. They've seen me take phone calls and put aside what I am doing for others in this me-culture. We are working hard at modeling a we-attitude. 1 Thessalonians 5:11 says, "Therefore encourage one another and build one another up, just as in fact you are doing."

Give authority where authority is. This means we obey whoever is in charge, wherever we are. Real leaders don't have to have all the answers, but they just know where to find them. Romans 13:2 says, "Therefore whoever resists the authorities resists what God has appointed . . ." (ESV).

Don't back down from a challenge. Is it hard? Will it cost? If it's worth the effort, then engage with all you've got. Success isn't outcomes, it's output. Philippians 4:13 says, "I can do all things through him who gives me strength."

Todd and I are actively learning both parenting and leadership aren't things that you ever really "figure out." It's just a bunch of listening and discernment, hoping how God created us and how He fills us is enough for the task at hand. These scripts simply remind us that at one point, truth hit us so hard that we decided to change the way we thought and lived. Some days, those memories and convictions can feel weak, and we need to be reminded of who we want to be. Reckless faith is choosing to be disciplined.

REFLECTION:

Whatever you do, work heartily, as for the Lord and not for men, knowing that from the Lord you will receive the inheritance as your reward. You are serving the Lord Christ.
– COLOSSIANS 3:23-24 (ESV)

What does this truth tell you about yourself? Others? God?

CHANGE:

What scripts do you have? What truths have hit you hard and changed how you live?

ACTION:

Write a script between yourself and someone important in your life (spouse, sibling, best friend, significant other) and hang it somewhere you will see it daily.

3 3

I Want to See the Light

Yes to Listening

The sign outside the building reads: "Dialogue in the Darkness." A girlfriend of mine and I joke that it must be a marriage counseling center. But it isn't. We are in Mexico, parent chaperones on a school field trip to a workshop on understanding people with disabilities. For an entire hour, during the course of this workshop, both children and adults are guided through a completely darkened building, making their way through various common circumstances people with vision challenges face in everyday life.

The facilitator tells us, "The most important rule is to listen for your guide. She will walk with you through the course, and she knows the path ahead. When she tells you to stop, *stop*! When she tells you to watch for the upcoming traffic, bridge, or other obstacle, take note."

Then we break into small groups, and my team receives its red-tipped canes. As we head into the large building, which is completely dark inside, one of the kids begins to cry and is escorted back to the light.

"What do you feel?" asks our guide. I think she means something different, but I can't help calling out, "Lost." She leads us through many common locales, including a grocery store, a "wooded" area with trees and unstable footing, a boat, and a restaurant. Most of the children are quiet, focusing on their next step. The only saving grace is the voice of the guide. She seems to be able to anticipate our moves before we do! She knows when to be encouraging and when to sternly direct our steps across a street. Sometimes, the other sounds threaten to drown out her voice, but she can always be heard if you strain or call out.

I couldn't help but see the spiritual application of this exercise. *Okay, okay, okay . . . I get it, Lord; I will listen better for Your voice*, I dialogue inside my head. Finally, an hour later, at the end of our experience and exhausted from the concentration it requires, we sit down with our guide while still in the darkness to process how we feel.

The children are full of comments:

"It was hard to not be able to just peek."

"I want to see the light."

"I was scared the whole time."

"I feel sorry for blind people."

I chip in, "I'm grateful you could see ahead and tell us what to expect."

"Well, that's funny," said the guide. "You didn't realize I'm actually blind—all the time, not just in here." Nobody says anything for a minute. She adds, "I've just learned how to listen for clues."

When Jesus called the disciples, they dropped their nets—their entire lives—and followed Him. When He calls us, we don't do much net dropping anymore, and sometimes we feel we can just keep doing what we've always been doing—only better with God at our side. But Jesus said in Mark 8:34, "Whoever wants to be my disciple must deny themselves and take up their cross and follow me." To follow the voice of the Guide is to let go of our own agenda and throw ourselves towards His, even if we can't see what's ahead. How much more reckless can you get than that?

There are moments when I feel like I am walking in the dark. The Bible talks about how the Word is a lamp unto my feet, and a lamp, when David wrote about it, would have only put out the light of a birthday candle. It wasn't a flashlight with a twenty-five-foot beam. It was enough light to illuminate just the step ahead. *Can I be ok with a faith journey I can only see one step at a time? Do I trust my Guide enough to walk me around or hold my hand through obstacles inevitably coming on my path? How good am I at listening?*

In the story of the showdown between Moses and Pharaoh over the future of the Israelites, one of the plagues that befell Egypt was darkness. The Bible says it was so dark, it could be felt.

Then the LORD said to Moses, "Stretch out your hand toward the sky so that darkness spreads over Egypt—darkness that can be felt."
So Moses stretched out his hand toward the sky, and total darkness covered all Egypt for three days. No one could see anyone else or move about for three days. Yet all the Israelites had light in the places where they lived.
— EXODUS 10:21-23

I love using my imagination and picturing thick darkness in the land. Yet God's people were with light wherever they lived? Like little human lighting bugs? How did it work? However it worked then, I think it's still true for God's people today. We can go into situations that feel dark, and threaten to overwhelm us, but He promises we'll have light with us, because *He* is light and *He* is with us. This means that no matter how hard my sin nature pulls down on me, I cannot be consumed.

Whether it's a situation where I've stepped out and gotten in over my head, or it's a parenting situation, or a financial need, or a marital conflict . . . there are dark storylines all around me. But if I open my Word, lift up my eyes, listen for my Guide, and step ahead, I can be confident He will never fail me, He will light my way.

REFLECTION:

I, the Lord, have called you in righteousness; I will take hold of your hand. I will keep you and will make you to be a covenant for the people and a light for the Gentiles, to open eyes that are blind, to free captives from prison and to release from the dungeon those who sit in darkness.
– ISAIAH 42:6–7

What does this tell you about yourself? Others? God?

CHANGE:

What does denying yourself look like to you? What does the darkness feel like to you?

ACTION:

Find a quiet and dark place and light a small candle. Pray and thank God for the small ways in which He is providing light for your next step.

34

Planting Tamarisk Trees
Yes to Inheritance

EXPERIENCE:

My great-grandmother, Lydia, was born in 1885 to a family without faith. She later came to know Jesus as a teenager, and eventually studied at Cleveland Bible College (today Malone University). There she met my great-grandfather, Martin, and together, after graduation, they started a church ministry in northern Ohio. The family lore is that he had the gift of serving and would often go to the local farms on Saturday and Sunday mornings, helping with chores, so the farmers and their families could attend services. Lydia, however, was the better speaker, and communicated in the pulpit in their conservative denomination on most Sundays.

They raised a family of four children, one of whom was my grandmother, Esther. She later birthed my father, Allen. His parents must have taught him the value of a woman's voice and spiritual discernment, because he always made room for mine while I was growing up.

Today, most Sundays you can find me in a church speaking, and I am sure it's in part because someone taught someone, who taught someone, who taught me—a woman has the ability to divide the Word of God. In a church culture often confused on this subject, I've always had a quiet confidence and I don't need to convince anyone or demand authority that isn't mine. I can humbly use my gifts and not look around for approval. Reckless faith is like that; its influence spans and inspires generations to come. I never met Lydia, but a small part of who I am today came from who she decided to be. What we do and how we spend our time and money will be known and patterned for those who come after us. God writes long storylines and understanding my place in them helps me keep the faith.

Rahab, the prostitute in the Bible who hid the Israelite spies, eventually married a Jew named Salmon and they birthed a son, Boaz. She had demonstrated herself to be a risk taker, intuitive, smart, and she sowed those seeds into her next generation. Boaz, understanding uniquely what challenges a woman on the outskirts of a community faced, was raised with eyes and a heart to notice a woman who came into his fields—Ruth. He extended to foreigners the kind of compassion and grace that was at one time extended to his mother. Rahab must have whispered in Boaz's ear a thousand times how God had protected them and would continue to. It was a part of his worldview, his understanding of how the Lord operated.

The love story of Ruth and Boaz is told in the book of Ruth, with Boaz, at times, working behind the scenes to provide and protect Ruth until she became his wife. Then the Lord enabled her to conceive, and she gave birth to a son. They named him Obed, and he became the father to Jesse. Jesse is the father of King David, a risk taker much like his great-grandparents Boaz and Ruth and great-great-grandparents Rahab and Salmon. By the time the family lore had been passed down to David, he had heard many stories of how the God of Israel had come through for his family over and over again. It was no wonder that, at such a young age, he picked up a slingshot and some stones to slay a giant.

The Bible teaches about a great cloud of witnesses, those who have gone before us, both in biblical history and in our own histories. They are cheering us on, from a place where it all now makes sense to them, and they are rooting for us to put our hope in an eternal future. What would they say to us about the subjects we spend so much time thinking and debating about? Where would they encourage us to invest, or how would they tell us to fight for freedom and peace?

Therefore, since we are surrounded by such a great cloud of witnesses, let us throw off everything that hinders and the sin that so easily entangles. And let us run with perseverance the race marked out for us, fixing our eyes on Jesus, the pioneer and perfecter of faith . . .
– HEBREWS 12:1-2

I don't know who is in your cloud of witnesses, but regardless of heritage, we have now all been grafted into God's tree. That means Abraham is in my family, Noah, Esther, David, they are in my family. The *chutzpah* (the Hebrew word for "audacity") of Rahab is a family characteristic. Peter's boldness can be yours. Mary's devotion is yours. God's family is ours, and they are cheering for us to look at life as it spans the generations and into eternity. We are a part of a very old story.

There is a tree that grows in Israel called the tamarisk tree. It doesn't fully bloom for sixty years, yet Abraham planted one in Genesis 21:33, "Abraham planted a tamarisk tree in Beersheba, and there he called on the name of the Lord, the Eternal God." This man, who had yet to see God's promises fulfilled, was determined to prepare for what he believed would still come. He planted those trees for his future generations' enjoyment.

Throughout my life, through my actions of faith, I have planted my own figurative tamarisk tree as a reminder and encouragement to generations ahead that God does move. Practically, that's hard. It means saving when

I would rather spend, and speaking when it's easier to be silent. It means resolving conflict when it's simpler to pretend, and investing in people when I might prefer free time. However, we get the privilege of being the someone who teaches someone who teaches someone who teaches truth to a generation yet to be, hungry to hear how faith can change everything.

REFLECTION:

Praise the Lord, for the Lord is good; sing praise to his name, for that is pleasant. For the Lord has chosen Jacob to be his own, Israel to be his treasured possession.
– PSALM 145:3-4

What does this teach you about yourself? Others? God?

CHANGE:

Who in your family has impacted how you see the world? How are you planting a tamarisk tree today?

ACTION:

Buy a tree or a flower and put it somewhere where you'll be reminded how important it is to invest in the next generation.

35

Set Out a Chair

Yes to Seeing the One

We were on a prayer walk, visiting families who receive services at Back2Back's Tres Reyes Community Center in Cancun. At each stop, we'd meet the members of the family and ask how we could pray for them. Typically, they'd mention provision, health needs, or broken relationships. The mother would share vulnerably, and, as we lifted her needs, a fragile connection would form.

As we entered Maria's house, she proudly introduced us to her two elementary-aged children, quick to share their academic successes and credit them for their hard work. Following her lead, they stood straight as she spoke, looking at us confidently. When she finished, someone asked how she found out about the center. She laughed, "That is a funny story."

An American staff member met her while walking in the community, and encouraged her to enroll her children in tutoring classes. She knew immediately she'd never do that, having a long-standing distrust of Americans. She also feared, due to her illiteracy, there would be forms she'd be embarrassed she couldn't fill out. She successfully avoided it for a while, but with her son falling behind in school, she eventually had nowhere else to turn. She came one afternoon to the community center, but insisted on standing outside of the classroom while her children participated. Although this meant long hours in the hot sun, she was more concerned with her children's safety.

Sandy, one of the teachers, could sense Maria listening to her teaching through a window. The next day, she left Maria a chair outside the door, a kind gesture so she could sit while the children were in class. Instead of resting, Maria sat on the edge of her seat. She was attentive, Sandy recognized, and possibly learning the material for the first time. The next morning, on her way into the classroom, Sandy quietly dropped a notebook on Maria's seat.

As Maria tells it, the lessons began to make sense, as she strung together letters to make words, and then words to read sentences. Eventually, she attended parenting classes where she learned about cooking, finance, and faith. "I don't want you to tell me what God says about me any-more," she told her Bible class, "Now that I can read, give me a Bible. I want to find out for myself."

"That was three years ago," she said, "And now, I have been baptized, and I share my faith journey regularly with my extended family and neighbors."

Maria's life looks different from just a few years ago. She makes items to sell in the market and competently sup-ports her family. She worships alongside her children. She admitted that she is not only working towards a future, she's trying to rebuild a broken past, "I was angry and scared, and God had so much waiting for me. Sometimes all we need to turn things around is an invitation."

Then Jesus told them this parable: "Suppose one of you has a hundred sheep and loses one of them. Doesn't he leave the ninety-nine in the open country and go after the lost sheep until he finds it? And when he finds it, he joyfully puts it on his shoulders and goes home. Then he calls his friends and neighbors together and says, 'Rejoice with me; I have found my lost sheep.'"

– LUKE 15:3-6

I have always been fascinated with this parable. I am in awe of a God who doesn't look at the ninety-nine and thinks He has pretty good odds. I often erroneously attribute human tendencies to God (like fatigue, or irrita-tion, or, in this case, meritocracy), and so I am amazed He doesn't just stick around in the midst of those ninety-nine and enjoy their fellowship. It's what I am tempted to do most days, be satisfied with "good enough." Instead, God has an eye that has never left the "one," who sees wherever it has scampered off to, either out of rebellion or in escape. He understands its story with all its complexity and in its entirety, and still is without judgment. He sees that the sheep is angry and scared, and He is compassionate. He sees its confusion and deception, and does not stop pursuit.

There has been a moment in every believer's life when we were that sheep around His shoulders; when He caught up with us and brought us home. What happens then? When we spend time around the other ninety-nine, there can be friction. At its best, the good kind of friction we label as accountability and iron sharpening iron. At its worst, it creates conflict and divides families, churches, friendships, marriages, and countries, and can cause even found sheep to wish they were lost again.

Maria landed in the middle of a community where people were concerned about her family's well-being. She first knew Christians before she knew Christ. They left an impression on her, stoking a curiosity and challenging what she previously thought was true. This is often how it works. The lost will sense God's love through God's people and be moved by it. It's our job then to make sure Maria looks through us to God, instead of to us for what we can never provide.

He interrupted what should have been the expected next events of Maria's story to redirect her path. It's what He does. In the Gospels, we read how He saw the Samaritan woman at a well, and used her testimony to impact a community. He saw a bleeding woman in need of a touch, and drew His attention to her healing. He saw an adulterous woman needing forgiveness and a crowd too critical to offer it, so He reached out. For Maria, He saw a desperate mom needing support, and He sent it through a teacher who offered a chair and a notebook.

REFLECTION:

Then Jesus told them this parable: "Suppose one of you has a hundred sheep and loses one of them. Doesn't he leave the ninety-nine in the open country and go after the lost sheep until he finds it? And when he finds it, he joyfully puts it on his shoulders and goes home. Then he calls his friends and neighbors together and says, 'Rejoice with me; I have found my lost sheep.'"
– LUKE 15:3-6

What does this tell you about yourself? Others? God?

CHANGE:

Where have you seen God intervene for you? Where did

God find you when He came after you?

ACTION:

Who is the "one" in your community God is revealing to you? How can you set out a chair for them today?

36

A Foundation of Faith

Yes to Authenticity

EXPERIENCE:

I hate hard. I don't like when friends divorce, people I love die, someone relapses, a child runs away. I don't like the feeling that, at any moment, the other shoe could drop. How, when we've all seen so many stories not go the way we wanted, can we still hold on to a reckless kind of faith?

I was diagnosed with the BRCA2 gene in 2016 and made the decision to prophylactically undergo a double mastectomy and hysterectomy. I remember telling the congregation where I serve, "This action of trying to out-run cancer in a foot race is not a guarantee of anything. I could get hit by a car or develop disease somewhere else." It wasn't insurance so that bad things couldn't happen to me, it was doing all I could and then handing God the rest.

God won't waste a thing. Even hard can be good, if it makes us more like Him. Todd and I said when this journey started, "If we do this well, we will be more like Christ on the other side." And I can joyfully attest that God used this season to remake and recreate me. I experienced plenty of conviction and had no excuse but to work through it with Him. Flat on my back, I was an eager student in His classroom and, for that alone, I would go through it all again.

During the recovery, I struggled to read my Bible. I couldn't focus on the words or sustain the attention needed for study. Normally, I think in rainbows and unicorns, but without a regular dose of Bible and Jesus, sometimes at night, I was thinking catastrophically, and I would wake up afraid. One night, knowing I needed Him, I picked up my phone on my nightstand, careful to not wake Todd. I opened up my Bible app, and noticed for the first time that there was an audio feature, so I hit play. I happened to have been in the Gospels, so it was mostly Jesus' words. I was in the dark, on the phone, and a man was reading Jesus' words to me . . . it was like Jesus was calling! The Word promises to heal, and I felt the peace needed to relax and fall back asleep. I began to use the audio Bible all throughout the following months, just another tool in my spiritual toolbelt.

Could my faith be reckless enough to first trust His ways are best and then think about my own needs? Could I grow faith strong enough (like a muscle), that when it has to pick up a heavy or difficult situation, I can easily lift it and still have hope? That doesn't mean I don't think about consequences and pain, that doesn't mean I don't doubt, but I layer those on top of faith instead of the other way around. When we try to lay our faith on top of our questions, it is an unstable foundation, and the weak foundation almost always cracks. When we have a base level of faith, the questions come, but don't insist on being answered.

There are some today who wave their unanswered questions as flags of honor, in the name of authenticity. They prefer to "be real" and broadcast their doubts rather than press in and cry to Jesus, like the man in Mark 9:24, "I believe; help my unbelief" (ESV). These outspoken believers dishonor God in an attempt to be "relatable." We have to first give God credit and admit we can't do anything on our own. I am concerned about messages going out from the church that say our futures are *ours* to determine, our abilities are only limited by our belief in *ourselves*. I don't believe in myself; I am, quite frankly, a hot mess. I believe in what God has said about me. It's through *Him* that all things are possible. And while I do think we need to pursue an authentic faith, we need to make sure that our doubts aren't seeping through our foundation of faith and destroying what God has worked with us to build. We strengthen our foundation of faith by spending time with God and reading His Word.

We all have stories we get involved in that don't turn

out with happy endings or with bows on them. Why do we feel so entitled to happy endings? *Instead of obsessing over happy endings could I just offer, obey, pray, hope, listen, lean in . . . and leave the rest to God?* God promises us our disappointments will not last forever. He turns things around, He brings us back, He takes us home. He rebuilds, restores, repairs. It is still in my nature to question and fight. I can return to the same question or same sin or same fear, and it results in further confusion. But now there is a difference. Now, instead of striving for happy endings, I strive for a reckless faith, a faith that promises me that God forgives me and has a plan, and His plan is the best. His plan is for eternity, and His purposes don't need to be revealed in the short term just so I feel better now.

Authenticity, when met with a foundation of faith, results in growth rather than destruction.

REFLECTION:

I know what I'm doing. I have it all planned out—plans to take care of you, not abandon you, plans to give you the future you hope for. When you call on me, when you come and pray to me, I'll listen. When you come looking for me, you'll find me . . . I'll make sure you won't be disappointed . . .
– JEREMIAH 29:11-14 (MSG)

What does this truth tell you about yourself? Others? God?

CHANGE:

What have you seen God rebuild? What passage can you take a moment to listen to with an audio Bible?

ACTION:

Write down any unanswered questions you currently have due to circumstances—say to God, "Your will be done," and then serve yourself communion. You are giving Him what isn't yours to carry while He gives you back grace and freedom.

37

Adding More Water
to the Beans
Yes to Vision

Rejected at birth, my friend Meme was passed on to a relative who treated her as a servant rather than a family member. She was also "loaned out" to neighbors for manual labor and was denied basic affection. When she was fourteen years old, she was married off to a widower more than a decade her senior, and while other teens were worried about their pimples and phone calls, she was giving birth and trying to survive, while her husband squandered their earnings.

I first met Meme while she was working at one of the

orphanages with her family. Her husband, the widower, had become a believer through an employer, and, a short time later, Meme came to Christ as well. Together, they served for more than a decade in the Christian children's home close to our house. After they left a few years back, I lost track of them.

One night, there was a knock at my door. "Beth, are you in there?" I hear a voice from outside.

"Meme!" I exclaim, opening the door. "It's been years. How you have been? What have you been doing?"

"I was wondering," she mutters humbly, "could I come in and offer my cleaning services? I'll exchange you work for food."

"Meme, you know I'd be happy just to give you some food, but if you really need work, we can figure something out."

We renew our friendship that day—and it's a friendship that has changed both our lives. I have given Meme employment and a decade and a half of discipleship, but what she has given me is far more impressive: her vision.

She voluntarily lives in a squatter village, staying there for more than twenty years, so she can share the gospel with those around her. *Voluntary poverty?* I have heard of such things, but I've never met someone who lived it out—until I met Meme. Meme sees people for who they are, not what they are, and, as clichéd as it sounds, that rarely happens. Through her example, I now see a prostitute as someone's daughter, a wife beater as an adult orphan, and a drunk as a desperate mother. She has taught us to look at the people we serve, who live in the most desperate of circumstances, in terms of their relationships, rather than their labels. And then, with a faith God built brick by brick with His own hands, I see Meme trust Him for provision and healing where most would throw up their hands (or at least wring them) and walk away. As a result, He provides and heals, and those relationships slowly walk toward restoration. There is an expression in Spanish when someone unexpected comes to dinner, you just "add more water to the beans." I've witnessed God Himself multiply Meme's "beans" to cover the needs that pile up on her doorstep. As we spend what we have on those in need, we store up for ourselves treasures in heaven. Although to the world Meme looks poor, she is one of the richest ladies I know.

It's too easy for those of us who work with the poor to forget to address their poverty. We work around them or on behalf of them, but often we still don't know how they live or how to help. We see missing dollars and think adding money will fix their situation, but financial poverty is just a symptom of what's going on. We have a responsibility to be God's hands and feet in their lives, for God cares about their hungry bellies, hurting feet, bug-infested beds, and runny noses. He cares about their broken marriages or lack of spiritual understanding and sees far more to heal than what we see with our eyes. If we march into orphanages and poverty-stricken communities and ignore the needs we find there, we will attract a few curious observers, but we'll make little impact. How can we see the complexity of what's going on? Where do we start if we feel called to bring *shalom* to their chaos?

Through the vision of someone like Meme, we are able to understand the daily struggles those in poverty face, and build relationships. It's harder to measure, messier to maintain, and makes our days more complicated, but it's through relationships that vision is born and eventually spread. It's how the healthy exchange between God's people and those He's reaching out to is done in a way that honors Him and dignifies everyone involved. This kind of vision comes from seeing through someone else's eyes, and not having a personal agenda.

Meme's example has taught me ministry isn't just your "day job" and *all* my moments can be ministry—eating, cooking, washing, watching children, anything I do beside someone else, for someone else, or with someone else. I'm trying to make ministry and breathing and walking in the Spirit all the same action.

When Meme showed up at my door years ago, offering to work in exchange for food, I had no idea that I'd one day minister alongside her, bringing the gospel and food and housing to people. But God knew.

God has ordained all of our days ahead of time (Psalm 139). He looked at Meme when she was only a small, abandoned girl—and He saw who she would be today. He saw her walking around her village with her Bible in one hand and provision in the other, sharing God's love and concern for those around her. That's vision!

REFLECTION:

Compassion doesn't originate in our bleeding hearts or moral sweat, but in God's mercy.
– ROMANS 9:16 (MSG)

What does this truth tell you about yourself? Others? God?

CHANGE:

Who has God led you to build a relationship with? How do you define poverty?

ACTION:

Invite someone over for a meal, and "adding more water to the beans," share what you have for the benefit of someone else.

38

How is the Story Going to End?

Yes to Holding On

A person who makes the wildest claims, has the biggest ideas, and can stir up the largest crowd usually ends up being labeled a "visionary." For me, a visionary is a person who has spent so much time with the Master, they see circumstances completely from His perspective. For instance, when they're told, "It can't be done," they build arks, part seas, and believe in virgin births. And when they look into the eyes of an orphan, they see the child of a King. That is vision!

I was a student at Indiana University, studying education, and it was my first day of classes in a new semester.

One of my professors began his lecture, "There are two kinds of learners in the world. Can anyone name them for me?" The professor drones on. As students, we are disappointed he didn't just pass out the syllabus and send us home. No one answers the question.

The professor tries another tactic, "If anyone can tell me what the two kinds of learners are, I will give them a passing grade without having to attend another class!"

Now he has my attention.

After we all painfully admit we have no idea, he continues his lecture with two questions: "How many of you would be willing to watch a movie without knowing how it's going to end?" Some hands raise, not mine. "And how many have no desire to volunteer for a committee or a group project until you have established the purpose and final outcome?" More hands raise, mine the highest.

"All right, then," he continues. "There are two kinds of learners: part-to-whole learners and whole-to-part. The faster you understand yourself, the way you teach, and the ways your students learn, the better off you'll be.

"A part-to-whole learner wants to solve the math problem meticulously, confidently knowing they've left nothing undone. The whole-to-part learner, by contrast, wonders, *When will I ever use this in real life?* A part-to-whole learner never reads the last page of a book first; he wants to ride the wave of suspense until the end. A whole-to-part learner won't read a book without a strong recommendation from someone and, even still, sometimes sneaks a look at the last page."

I am a whole-to-part learner. I want to know *the point* of something before I commit to it. I want to know where things are headed before I jump on board. So, imagine my learning curve when I confronted this fact: having "vision" means listening to the Lord and taking the next step in faith. Many people teach vision is being able to see further ahead than the other guy, but I've found it's just the opposite: vision is not knowing the end game ahead of time.

Having vision means experiencing growth. In ten years, I'll pick up this book, shake my head, and think, *If only I knew then what I know now.* Having vision, listening to God, and stepping out in faith all mean my life experiences are building within me principles I need for God's next call. They are the path I'm being led along—a path whose end I cannot see. For instance, when we moved to Mexico, we prayed simply, *"Lord, we ask that fifty people will come visit us this year to serve alongside us in ministry."* That seemed an unattainable figure. By the end of that first year, however, over 350 people had visited us. Our vision was nothing compared to God's!

Too often people think of the pastor with the largest congregation as the true visionary, while another pastor, who has ministered to the same small group year after year, is seen as stuck or stagnant. Of course, the opposite can just as easily be true. The faithful pastor of a small church might have the greatest vision for his flock, while the megachurch pastor might easily be a good speaker and little more. God's idea of vision isn't about numbers. The foster mom who believes in the value of the difficult child placed in her care might have more vision than the head of a large and thriving children's ministry.

So, what is vision if it's not big plans and big ideas? Vision is listening to the Lord and taking the next step. It's trusting where He's leading is better than any plan you could dream up on a whiteboard. Vision is keeping to the plumb line and not veering off when something shiny comes along. Vision is about relationship, not about capacity, or ability, or projection. It's a reckless faith that sees God instead of a crowd or a score.

It's a reckless faith that believes in what isn't seen. It believes there is always more than one mission going on at a time and isn't flustered when the next step feels like a misstep. Patiently, peacefully, we are to hold on, wait, remember, trust, listen, and believe. It's in the holding on, it starts to get really good.

REFLECTION:

For still the vision awaits its appointed time; it hastens to the end—it will not lie. If it seems slow, wait for it; it will surely come; it will not delay.
– HABAKKUK 2:3 (ESV)

What does this truth tell you about yourself? Others? God?

CHANGE:

What is your idea of vision? Who have you seen effectively share a vision God's given them?

ACTION:

Get out a piece of paper and write your younger self a letter. What do you wish you had known then that you know now?

39

Letting Go and Being Led

Yes to Commitment

My friend Juan sits down with me on the bench. "So, how often do you actually enjoy a committee meeting?" he asks.

"Not often, unless I'm running it, I guess," I laugh, wondering what he means.

"Well, I just went to my weekly meeting with the woman who is planning the city-wide youth rally," he says, "but we're hitting some roadblocks. People aren't doing their assignments; there are delays in contracts. It's been frustrating. There are a lot of great people on the committee, and the leader has a good plan, but we're all feeling uninspired, and she could tell."

I laugh and say, "Sounds like lots of meetings I've been to."

"But then she asked us what we think she's doing wrong. It was really quite brave. I told her, 'I don't feel like you've allowed us to share in the vision. It's so "all yours" I feel like I'm doing you a favor, which is fine, but that'll only take me so far. If I'm allowed to own the vision with you, and see how we're working toward a plan God has put on *our* hearts, I will work until I am bone tired and my fingers are bleeding. I'm sorry, it's just my heart to work for God has a greater capacity than my hope you appreciate my efforts.'"

"Did everything get quiet after you said that?" I ask.

"For a minute, until she realized what I said had some truth, and now we're all going to pray about the plans and meet again next week. I'm looking forward to a meeting I was previously dreading."

If the new vision is from God, then everyone involved will know it. To let go of control is to give birth to vision.

Communion is just a snack unless you purpose to remember the Holy Spirit while you're eating and drinking. Washing someone's feet is just bathing unless you invite supernatural humility into the act. Worship can easily be relegated to singing when you forget the One on whom to focus. Baptism is only a symbolic swim if in your heart you don't believe you are now identifying with Christ. Praying is just poetry—or pleading—unless you believe someone is listening. Vision is just planning ahead unless you take direction from the Lord.

And perhaps that is the most reckless act of faith yet.

It requires a letting go of our vision, our plans, our idea of what's good, big, best. A reckless faith trusts when God leads us down an unknown or lesser-desired path. It trusts the relationships we want to let go of—because they're too hard or too complicated—are actually being used for His glory, for our sharpening, and for the others' good. It trusts this change, though difficult, is right because God sees farther down the path than we do. Vision is the natural byproduct of reckless faith because it's a choice to see ourselves as being woven into a bigger tapestry than we can see today.

The vision starts and ends with God. It's not something we can muster up ourselves or dream up in our offices or committees. It's putting God's voice on the highest volume in our heads—and then letting go and being led.

So what's next as God pours Himself out on behalf of the millions of orphans worldwide? How do we address economic issues, healthcare, adoption? Do we need more agencies? Churches? Missionaries? Materials? Awareness? Dollars?

Some plotlines in the next chapter of my life I'm sure of. For instance, more and more people will commit their lives to orphan care—since it's a problem that is growing and warrants an entire movement—and more miraculous provisions will appear, more lives will be redeemed, more

God-sized dreams will be dreamed. There will also be more heartbreak, more needs than we can meet, more children abandoned, more failed classes, and more missed opportunities. But I can promise you, in the next chapter, those of us who work in this ministry won't stop until God tells us to. We will continue to fight and pray (and continue to invite you to do so as well) for the marginalized and abandoned children. We will serve children—sweating for them, defending them, and standing beside them—in the name of Jesus. Please join us as we stay up late talking, worrying, praying for and with the child whose Spirit is "waking up." Cry and laugh with us at the children's antics and delight with us in their successes. They need discipline, with consistency and humility, while they test their boundaries.

Will you commit with us to provide them a home and lead them out of the darkness and loneliness? Will you be used by God to vindicate them, and, every once in a while, watch one be literally rescued?

Today we stand together and commit to share not only the gospel, but our lives, as children watch us fall down, sin, celebrate, laugh, risk . . . But we will not leave them, not until they ask to be left alone—and even then, we'll keep pursuing them.

As God leads us, we will come to them, hear them, lift them up, and be their parents. We will never forget that they matter to God and were created for a purpose and have a unique destiny. We will extend mercy toward them and be the recipients of their grace. We will give them food and clothing and be their helpers (in chores, in deciding which outfit to wear, in finding the right medicine, in thinking through their future). We will incline our ears, we will lift them up in prayer, and we will maintain their cause—not just until we are tired or embarrassed or uncomfortable, not just until we don't feel like it anymore—but we will maintain their cause until God comes again to bring us home.

REFLECTION:

Because we loved you so much, we were delighted to share with you not only the gospel of God but our lives as well.
– 1 THESSALONIANS 2:8

What does this truth tell you about yourself? Others? God?

CHANGE:

Where have you had to let go of control on an idea, project, or relationship? How can you commit to the cause of the orphan?

ACTION:

Learn something new about the fatherless in your own city.

40

Only Wholeness and Belonging

Yes to Renewal

Todd and I are always being asked how many cities we'd like to be doing ministry in ten years from now. I could strike a "visionary pose" and say, "I hope we'll be in ten new cities, serving ten thousand orphans with a staff of a thousand." People might then shake their heads and sigh, "Wow! What vision she has . . ."

But that's crazy.

I have no idea if God will multiply this ministry or raise up another to minister to orphans. I have no idea if He will call us to go miles deeper where we are, or miles wider where we aren't. I do know He rarely reveals the whole story, which we whole-to-parters find so unsatisfying. He's much more interested in the development of my dependence on Him and my relationship with Him than He is in impressing me with His plans. I already know He has big plans. He has an incredible track record. So how much longer will we do this work? I don't know. When I give my usual answer, "Until we're called otherwise," people smile because it sounds so spiritual.

The truth is there are days (like today) when things don't get wrapped up in a bow, when there are more disappointments than victories, when I want to pack up and go "home." But for now, this is my home. No place on earth is really supposed to be home anyway; we are to be uncomfortable and restless until we are called to our eternal home.

Vision is tonight I will continue to listen to the Lord and to feel His passion for the orphaned child run through my heart.

Vision is a peace today that I have done all He created me to do.

Vision believes I will wake up tomorrow and be used by Him again. It is seeing every person's God-given potential and birthright.

Vision is waiting and watching and knowing God will repay the years the locusts have eaten.

Vision is crying out for solutions to problems that are bigger than I can solve and knowing He will answer.

Vision is investing myself in lives that will blossom long after I've left the scene.

Vision is hope and faith in a God I cannot see, but who I believe has ordained my days and is working out all things according to His good purpose and will.

So how is vision accomplished? Not by doing or seeing, which always gets so much credit. It's by listening to His voice and obeying.

I think it's remarkably fitting the Lord ends His sixty-six-chapter book of education for us with a vision. It has been a source of conflict in the church, but Revelation is just that, a revelation of a time when God's vision will come to pass. I'm looking forward to that day when I am out of work, for we who know God will be adopted into His kingdom. There will be no orphans—only wholeness and belonging. Until that day, we trust in God and in His mercy and extravagant love.

May He continue to show up—and show off—for His children.

REFLECTION:

Then I saw "a new heaven and a new earth," for the first heaven and the first earth had passed away, and there was no longer any sea. I saw the Holy City, the new Jerusalem, coming down out of heaven from God, prepared as a bride beautifully dressed for her husband. And I heard a loud voice from the throne saying, "Look! God's dwell-

ing place is now among the people, and he will dwell with them. They will be his people, and God himself will be with them and be their God. 'He will wipe every tear from their eyes. There will be no more death' or mourning or crying or pain, for the old order of things has passed away." He who was seated on the throne said, "I am making everything new!" Then he said, "Write this down, for these words are trustworthy and true." He said to me: "It is done. I am the Alpha and the Omega, the Beginning and the End. To the thirsty I will give water without cost from the spring of the water of life. Those who are victorious will inherit all this, and I will be their God and they will be my children."

– REVELATION 21:1–7

What does this tell you about yourself? Others? God?

CHANGE:

How do you hear from God? What does renewal feel like to you?

ACTION:

Take note of the last forty days of "Action" and see if there were any themes. Think about all the ways you said *yes* to God. Where did the Spirit speak to you? Tell a friend and encourage them to challenge you to take more steps in this direction.

A Note to the Reader

Thank you for taking this journey, it's my prayer you've learned more about yourself, others, and the Lord. I would love to hear where the challenges took you and how this season of renewal has prepared you for what's to come. I hope forty days later, the pattern of experiences, reflections, changes, and actions have become a part of your daily rhythm.

I am forever drawn to a reckless faith, because it isn't fake and it doesn't pretend. It feels deeply and lives fully. It tells the truth. It asks questions, cries out, and tests boundaries. It has a conversation with God in a dynamic way, not a static way. It molds its understanding as it encounters new situations and experiences new growth. That's the adventure a reckless faith promises.

"God has a plan" is not a cliché or Band-Aid you put on wounds that aren't healing. "God has a plan" is a mantra for a way of life that says you don't have to have all the answers to proceed. You can throw yourself towards the Red Sea and if it opens, praise God! You knew it!

How does it open? Why does it open now and didn't earlier? Why did it close on the Egyptians? To those questions, we can apply a faith that believes God is good, He is sovereign and is to be trusted. Not in mindless obedience, but with child-like faith.

This child-like, reckless faith will take us to places and into relationships we can't yet imagine, and will allow us to be reintroduced over and over again to the love of Jesus.

I will pray the Spirit continues to captivate us all.

Acknowledgements

I want to thank the staff at Back2Back Ministries, who cheered me on during this project, and read drafts, offered suggestions, and listened to stories. I especially want to thank Jenna Ghizas, who multiplies my efforts and has a spirit of yes about her. Onward Christian Soldier!

I want to thank Martha and Ann, who lifted me up and shared their lives so generously. Your investment in my life is immeasurable . . . Here's to more Diet Cokes and international adventures.

To the people whose stories are told in these pages, I stand in awe of how God manifested Himself through your life. Thank you for living brave.

To friends who challenge and encourage me, take my calls, and meet me where I am: the longer I am on this journey, the more grateful I am for you.

To my family in every direction, thank you for cultivating a culture of vulnerability and teachability and being open to our stories being shared. I love each and every one of you. You all are the richest expression of God's blessing I know.

To Todd, the only one who has lived these stories alongside of me. How does it keep getting better every year? Thank you for being my deepest breath of the day.

Notes

Notes

Notes

Notes

Notes

Notes

_____

_____

_____

_____

_____

_____

_____

_____

_____

_____

_____

_____

_____

_____

_____

_____

Notes

Notes

Notes

Notes

Notes

Notes

Notes

Notes

Notes

Notes

Notes

Notes

Notes

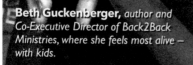

Beth Guckenberger, *author and Co-Executive Director of Back2Back Ministries, where she feels most alive — with kids.*

You.
You have this one precious life.

Every day, you choose how to invest your time… your life. Some days, you invest in friends. Some days, you invest in family. Some days, you invest in community. Some days, you invest in you.

And some days…
you feel a holy desire – the desire to invest in something new. Something that grows your world perspective, that serves, that loves, that gives. Something that makes you feel alive. And perhaps, you have felt a stirring, a joy, a yearning to remain a part of the story.

There is more.
Be inspired. Consider a next step. Learn how you can join a movement of change.
back2back.org/40days

BACK2BACK
MINISTRIES